Harold W. Sundstrom
Mary O. Sundstrom

Collies

How to Take Care of Them and to Understand Them

Drawings by Michele Earle-Bridges
Consulting Editor: Fredric L. Frye, DVM, MSC, FRSM

BARRON'S

Contents

Preface

Hardly a generation passes that does not fall in love with the collie; no other breed has so captured the public's affection. A delightful sense of humor and intense loyalty have made the collie a welcome member in all types of families. The beauty and character qualities of the collie have for years provided inspiration to writers and artists, and the collie has a legendary reputation, both on and off the television and movie screen. The collie's integrity and courage are part of an honored heritage. Of all the breeds, the collie is the dog most often written about.

The collie's intelligence and love for mankind are matters of longstanding record. Superlative as a sentinel or messenger, proven in two world wars, experiences showed that it cannot be trained to attack a human being on command, without direct provocation. The collie's readiness to defend its family, on the other hand, has been demonstrated by countless, well-attested incidents. Collie heroics are accepted as almost standard performance and the collie has been named repeatedly in the national dog hero awards given each year. In fact, no other breed has won the coveted honor more than the collie.

The modern collie is faithful to this tradition. It embodies all the legendary qualities, and the sight of such a dog makes an unforgettable impression. The storied past of the collie enhance its reputation as the ideal home companion and great friend of children.

In this manual, you will learn about the exceptional characteristics of collies, how to care for them, train them, breed them, and show them.

Beautiful color photos and informative drawings will make this a wonderful guide to enjoying your collie.

The authors of this pet book and the editors of Barron's Pet Owners Manuals wish you great pleasure with your collie.

History of the Collie

Collies originated in the border area of Scotland and England.

Rough and smooth varieties of collie have the same kind temperament and intelligence.

Origin

The collie's origin in the border area of Scotland and northern England was evolutionary. Though its early history is vague, breed historians suppose that dogs introduced by the Roman invaders about 500 B.C. eventually bred with local herding dogs. Later, the agricultural revolution of the mid-eighteenth century gave rise to the selective breeding of domestic animals. When farm animals were confined to walled or fenced pastures, this move from open fields to enclosures had a marked effect on both livestock and the breeding of farmers' dogs. Among other shepherd-type dogs, two varieties of collies evolved—the rough- and the smooth-coated collie. The collies were used for herding and as guardians and later as companions and show dogs. With broad, short heads and heavy ears, the early collies were smaller than the modern one that began to emerge around 1886.

Rough and Smooth Varieties

In addition to the well-known "Lassie"-type of collie, there is a smooth variety. In smooth collies the coat is short and dense, and requires much less grooming. Sometimes, smooth collies may appear smaller because of the difference in coat, but they are actually identical to their rough brothers and sisters and have the same kindly temperament and intelligence.

It is an open question whether the smooth collie was a parallel development of the rough collie or was developed as a separate breed. The rough specialized in sheep, while the smooth

Sable-headed white rough collie.

was used extensively with cattle. Generations of careful breeding have turned the collie into the beautiful specimen it is today, with the rough's elegant coat and the smooth's distinctive outline, increased size, and tulip ears. Both the smooth and the rough have the same structure, characteristics, and temperaments. Breed historians declare that during the mid-1800s northern England's smooth collies resembled the present type more closely than the rough collie. Once used as a herder and drover of sheep and cattle to market, the smooth-coated collie of today is a descendant of one of the oldest types of pastoral dogs.

"Colley Dog"

Many of the early collies were black and white in color. It was believed that less white color denoted the purity of the breed. The darkness of the breed's coat may have derived from the Anglo-Saxon word for black—"col." The collie's name was originally spelled "colley." Scotland's black-faced sheep were once called "colleys," and the dog that herded them and drove them came to be known as "colley dog." William Shakespeare used the word in its meaning of black in reference to the "collied night" in *A Midsummer Night's Dream.* "Coll, our dog" was mentioned by Geoffrey Chaucer, who is the source for the word coal. Other writers have suggested that the white band around the collie's neck is a natural collar. Another historian has said that the word collie is derived from the Gaelic tongue, since the word for a whelp or puppy is *cuilean* in that ancient language.

The Popular Collie

From the Scottish lowlands where it originated and has a long history as a herding dog, the collie emerged as a distinct and popular purebred dog in the middle of the nineteenth century.

England's Queen Victoria became enamored of the collie and claimed the breed as a companion dog at Scotland's Balmoral Castle. Returning to London with the royal family, the breed gained wide popular acceptance and began its ascendancy as a favored dog in both the United Kingdom and abroad.

Collies in America

Collies used for herding and guarding were brought to America and Canada by migrating settlers for use on farms and ranches.

Collies gained great public favor as companion dogs in the United States and were tremendously successful on the show dog circuit. Benefiting one of the oldest breeds, the Collie Club of America was organized in 1886 as the national parent club and became a member of the American Kennel Club in 1888.

Inevitably, collies imported from Great Britain were the basis of American breeding stock and provided the majority of show dog entries in subsequent decades. The most famous collie fancier at the turn of the century was financier and industrialist J. Pierpont Morgan. His Cragston Kennels cut a wide swath in the awards at the biggest American shows in the 1890s. By the end of World War I, domestic collie breeders were primary in the show ring.

Book, Movie, and TV Fame

The collie's reputation in America became fixed in public popularity with its immortalization on the pages of Albert Payson Terhune's novels, articles, and short stories about his Sunnybank collies early in this century. Terhune's glowing prose in books titled *Bruce, Lad: A Dog,* and *Grey Dawn,* fixed in the public's eye the vision of the collie as a dog of unquestioned courage and intelligence,

Consider carefully the name you give your collie if it is to be registered with the American Kennel Club. This name may be different than his "call name." The longer and more unusual name is more likely to be approved than, for example, a plain "Blaze" or "Rex."

as well as an uncanny understanding of humans.

The contemporary collie's popularity soared worldwide with the beloved 1945 technicolor adventure film classic, *Lassie Come Home.* British author Eric Knight's novel was the collie star's first movie and was followed by a succession of Lassie films. Both Terhune and Knight described the collie "as loyal a dog as you will ever know." From their pages and through movies and, later, television, the collie has become an American folk hero.

Perhaps the collie's greatest popularity occurred with the globally serialized television programs featuring a succession of "Lassies." Trained by the late Rudd Weatherwax, the Lassie-Weatherwax tradition continues with his son, Rob, who is now preparing yet another Lassie for film and television stardom.

The Collie Companion

Collie owners vouch for the breed's keen sense of understanding. They are gregarious and inquisitive by nature, and masters at playfulness and pranks. Like many of the herding breeds, collies have exceptional intelligence and sterling character. They excel as faithful, gentle, sweet-natured dogs with a great depth of affection. They love people and have a renowned willingness to bestow affection with an inherent desire to please. Admirers of collies are drawn to their tolerant nature.

Halamar's the Patriot was a large sable and white collie that decided early in life he was to be our gatekeeper. He rarely barked or made any type of sound. We believed he knew his very size made it unnecessary. Anyone could come into the yard and get almost to the door before Pat would make his presence known. He merely appeared to the guest and took his or her arm gently in his mouth,

making it very clear he wished the person to remain still until one of us said it was all right to enter. The routine would repeat itself when the person left our house, unless we walked our guest through the door and to his or her car. He never growled or was aggressive; indeed, he wagged his tail, pleased that he had accomplished a great task.

Collies are by no means timid dogs. Sensing imminent danger, they are instantly alert. It is not unusual—and a shared disposition with other breeds— to hear reports confirming collies' unerring awareness of thunderstorms hours before the sky hints of approaching heavy weather. Unusual restless and nervous actions accompanied by fast breathing are collies' unfailing telltale signs of looming storms and of earthquakes. We had such a collie at one time; ironically, her name was Halamar's Stormy Dawn.

Although collies are a large breed— females are 22 to 24 inches at the shoulder and males 24 to 26 inches— they do not require a large amount of space to feel at home—but they do

Collies like the famous Lassie have been popular in books, movies, and television stories for many years.

A collie is a loyal friend that enriches the life of its owner.

need an occasional romp or at least a daily walk. Coupled with the exercise that is a boon to both of you, teaching your collie to walk or run on leash is of benefit to all.

There is an indisputable reward for the collie owner: a collie is a friend who makes a human feel totally acceptable. Nothing can make you feel prouder than a neighbor or stranger stopping to greet your collie, exclaiming how lovely it is and how lucky you are. The only thing better than owning a collie is owning two.

Sable and white smooth collie.

Collie Puppies

How to Find Your Puppy

Locating a collie puppy can sometimes be a frustrating experience depending on your location and, in some cases, the time of year you begin your search. Newspapers are the most commonly used source. Those in large metropolitan areas will provide more ads than small town and rural papers and occasionally, in some areas, no collie advertising will be found. There are several other good alternatives to consider:

• Asking local veterinarians for a breeder reference will give you a head start in the right direction. Presumably, he or she will have knowledge of such breeders, having seen and treated their dogs.

• Another suggestion is to check an area all-breed kennel club, sometimes listed in the telephone book yellow pages. Their representative can put you in touch with member collie breeders or tell you about an area Collie Club.

• Another source is the American Kennel Club in New York (see "Useful Addresses" on page 90). They will put you in touch with the Collie Club of America who will give you information on breeders in your state.

No matter how you begin locating your collie puppy, good references are important. Talking to knowledgeable people, attending local dog shows and obedience trials, and asking questions about collies in general will be of help to you in finding and selecting the right puppy.

Sometimes you must be prepared to wait for a puppy. For instance, you may be referred to an excellent breeder in your area who may not have puppies at the time you call but is expecting a litter shortly or has planned a breeding for puppies to be born within several months. In that case, you can ask to be put on a waiting list. It is not unusual for such a breeder to ask for a deposit or to ask that you call back at the time the puppies are due. Be sure you understand the conditions of the deposit if you choose this option. When a breeder does not have puppies and does not have a litter planned in the near future, he or she will usually give you the name of someone with puppies for sale. Most breeders do not sell their puppies just before Christmas, as young pups require a lot of attention and often do not do well with all the bustle of holiday festivities.

If you are not looking for a young puppy, some breeders have older puppies and dogs they want to place in good homes. Younger puppies require a great deal of concentrated care. Therefore, an older one may be a good choice in homes where there are very young children or where both adults are away for a good part of the day.

Another excellent place to consider acquiring a collie is a collie rescue league. These dogs have been offered foster homes while permanent homes are being sought. Collie breeders and friends of the breed take collies into their homes for a variety of reasons. Many collies in this program are older dogs but there are numerous happy stories of how successful this alliance has proved to be. To find out about collie rescue programs, contact community animal shelters, the newspaper classified section offering pets for sale, local breeders, and veterinarians. There are collie rescue programs all across the United States.

Purchasing any dog should be viewed as a long term commitment and should not be done on a whim. A loyal and loving companion over a lifespan of many years should be your goal. An informed and knowledgeable buyer is an important factor in achieving this objective.

Before contact is made with the kennel or breeder that has puppies for sale, there are a number of questions you should ask:
• Will this be a collie for the entire family?
• Is this the breed everyone has agreed upon?
• Have you factored into the family budget the cost of veterinarian care, food, toys, leash, collar, grooming tools, training classes, boarding fees, or home care when the family takes a vacation without the dog?
• Who will be the primary caregiver, responsible for feeding, exercise, and cleaning up?

Male or Female?

Sometimes there is a strong preference for a puppy of one gender or the other. Both sexes make excellent companions and having a closed mind on the subject can limit your choices and cause you to pass over an excellent pup for that reason alone. Unless you intend to enter the world of show dogs and are entertaining thoughts of becoming a breeder—both areas better left to knowledgeable persons in the field—keeping your options open for both sex and color will bring your search for a puppy to a faster conclusion. Selecting a puppy on the merits of personality and temperament should please you more in the long run.

Dogs' nutritional requirements vary. Their basic needs depend largely on size, activity, and metabolism.

Whichever sex you choose, spaying or neutering at an appropriate age should be a serious consideration. This procedure does not affect the personality or the behavior in any significant manner. Talking with a veterinarian about this option before purchasing a dog of any age is a good idea. Many breeders today will ask that new owners do alter their puppies to prevent unwanted litters and indiscriminate breeding, contributing to the problem of overpopulation.

Females that are not spayed will come into season approximately every six months. A season or heat lasts for three weeks or twenty-one days. Close supervision must be given during this time as the scent of a female dog in heat attracts male dogs from near and far with only one objective in mind. Males that are not altered tend to want to roam further from home.

Both male and female collies alike grow up to be gentle and loving companions with an innate desire to please. Males are usually larger in size than their sisters but by only a few inches. Both sexes will shed their coats at least once a year and both will need a weekly grooming to keep them looking their best.

Whether male or female, the collie's natural curiosity will cause it to put its long nose in all your projects, inside or out. Both sexes take on the responsibility of their people family very seriously. While not aggressive in temperament, they seem always to be aware of their surroundings and they like things to be in good order. A yard full of playing children will be well cared for under the watchful eye of the family collie. Our children grew up with a collie as their protector, teacher, and friend. Neighborhood children often came to play during the day and our collie added them to her list of responsibilities. One day I heard the dog barking in almost a panic-like distress.

I went to the yard to see the mother of one of the children trying to pick up her child to take her home. The dog was circling the woman, getting between the child and herself. When I assured our collie that it was all right, she calmed down and seemed apologetic for her mistake. She, of course, had done the right thing and both the child's mother and I were pleased with her response. From then on, when the mothers came to collect their children, they let me know first.

Variety of Coats and Colors

In collies there are two coat varieties and four recognized colors.

Rough coat and smooth coat denote the length of coat on a collie, rough being longer and fuller and the most common, and smooth indicating a short-hair coat.

Colors: Both varieties of coats come in one of the four colors. The most common is sable or sable and white. This color encompasses all shades of brown from deep mahogany to light gold. Then there is the tricolor or black with white and tan markings. Blue merle is one of the least commonly seen colors but it is growing in popularity. Primarily light or dark gray with shades of black throughout the coat, this color is one of the most challenging patterns to achieve by collie breeders. It has been said that there are not two blue merles the same in coat color patterns. Another coat color more rarely seen is the white. White-coated collies have either sable, tricolor or blue merle-colored heads. The body coat is white, usually with some spots on the body that are the same color as those on the head.

Collar: Almost all collies have a white collar or at least a partial white collar—white on the chest, some white on the legs, white paws, and tail tip. Sometimes a white blaze, which may or may not disappear as the dog

Puppy picking may not always be easy, but it is always rewarding.

grows older, may be present on the face. No preference is given in color except by the owners and/or breeders. Breeding for a particular coat color is a genetic science and must be studied carefully to obtain the correct results.

Looking at a litter of puppies with two or more coat colors in evidence can be confusing at first, especially if you are not acquainted with the various colors. A litter may have both smooth and rough varieties of puppies. The breeder will quickly point out the difference to you as very young pups do not always have a sufficient amount of coat for you to easily determine which is which. No matter what color or variety you choose, a litter of collie puppies is a sight you will long remember.

Selecting the Right One

Now that you know a collie is the dog for you, and you have located a kennel or breeder with a litter of puppies for you to look at, and are armed with some knowledge about the breed, the selection process begins. Keep in mind that if you do not see

Admirers of the collie are drawn to its tolerant nature.

just what you like or for any reason have doubts about the breeder or person with whom you are dealing, do not hesitate to look further. While all puppies are appealing, you must feel satisfied in your own mind that this is the one for you, remembering that a little puppy grows into a big dog—for life.

Choosing an outgoing puppy, one that comes to you out of curiosity, one that seems confident of him- or herself with littermates as well as alone, should indicate a secure and happy pup. A young pup with bright eyes, healthy looking coat, and a good weight will tell you that it is off to a fine start. Do not buy a puppy until it is at least eight weeks old; puppies are not ready to make the social adjustment needed to leave their siblings before that age.

Most reputable breeders want good and loving homes for their puppies. A lot of thought, work, and care have gone into these animals. Even though you have a list of questions for the

seller, don't be surprised if he or she also has some questions about you.

Questions to the Seller

When the initial contact is made with the person selling puppies, a few questions from you are appropriate:
• Ask what were the ages and sexes in the litter?
• How many pups were in the litter?
• Are both the sire and dam purebred and/or registered with the American Kennel Club? (A registered dog means only that it is purebred, not that it is in any way endorsed by the American Kennel Club.)
• Can you see one or both of the parents? If not, why not?

You should follow with these pertinent queries:
• Have the pups received any inoculations?
• Have they been wormed or tested for worms?
• Have the eyes been checked by a qualified canine ophthalmologist for collie eye problems?

Price may or may not be discussed at this time. If you know how much you are willing to pay, this is the time to find out if these puppies fit into your budget.

If you are inquiring about an older puppy or a grown dog, the same questions with some modifications would apply. For instance, you might ask why this collie has not already been sold, or whether the dog has had some training to enable it to become a good family member, such as housebreaking and walking with a leash. Often, a puppy is kept by the breeder to watch as a show prospect, but not every puppy grows up to be a show dog or one suitable for breeding. These dogs are often beautiful examples of the breed but for various reasons they are not acceptable for show or breeding purposes and must therefore be sold.

When you are satisfied with the answers to your questions, set up an appointment to visit the seller and the puppies. Be prepared to spend some time looking at them, finding out what to expect if you decide to purchase one from this litter.

The Paper Trail

The puppy is yours! If you have purchased a registered AKC collie puppy, there will be papers to obtain and sign. The breeder will have already registered the puppy as part of a litter resulting from the mating of two purebred registered collies.

"Blue slip": Each puppy in the litter has its own "blue slip" with a litter registration number. You must be given this "blue slip" when you pay for your puppy unless there is a contract with stipulations to be fulfilled before the papers are given to you. In either case, the owner of the litter must sign the back of the slip stating that the puppy represented on the front has been sold or transferred to you, the date of the sale, or date the contract commitments are met. If you wish to register the puppy with the American Kennel Club as an individual collie, showing the name you give it with you as the owner, you must sign and complete the "blue slip" and return it with a fee to the American Kennel Club.

Pedigree form: The seller will also provide you with a pedigree form showing the lineage of your puppy with the names of the collies in its family. This is not a legal document but should be signed by the breeder as being accurate. Both the registration and pedigree are especially important papers for you to have if you are buying a show prospect puppy or one to be used for breeding.

A litter of collie puppies is a sight long remembered.

Medical record: A medical record showing dates of inoculations, fecal examinations and results, along with the eye examination report and name of the canine ophthalmologist and veterinarian used, should be given to you at the time of purchase. You may certainly ask for this information to be given in writing. Asking about the general health and longevity of the parents is of some interest but does not necessarily carry over to the offspring.

Diets: Since puppies have special needs and requirements regarding their diets, a feeding schedule noting the names of puppy foods, supplements, and amounts to feed are often supplied to the buyer to avoid tummy upsets for the first few days. Ask if the seller will guarantee the health of your puppy for 24 hours—until you can get to your own veterinarian for a checkup. Most sellers are glad to do this but be reasonable about the length of time you request. After all, sellers have no control over the puppy once it leaves their yard. Papers and puppy in hand, a new, wonderful adventure awaits you.

Puppy Care

First Days Home

Being prepared to transport your collie puppy to its new home will help make the move easier for everyone. If you have a dog carrier, put shredded newspaper in the bottom, along with a bath towel or small blanket. Be sure the carrier is well ventilated. Place the puppy gently into the carrier, reassuring it with a calm voice. The pup may protest for a few minutes, but if the ride home is relatively smooth, it may fall asleep. Holding the puppy on your lap or close to your side, if you do not have a carrier, will keep it from moving around or falling. The unfamiliar motion of the car could upset its stomach or make it feel nauseated, so put a towel beneath it and keep some paper towels handy. Upon arrival, put the puppy on the ground to relieve itself. Keep a watchful eye, as this will take several minutes while it sniffs the new territory.

When you buy a dog carrier for your puppy, remember how much it may grow.

Before bringing your puppy home, you should decide where it will sleep and spend time when unsupervised. Giving the puppy the run of the whole house is bewildering for a young dog. An indoor pen or enclosure of some sort, where the puppy will feel secure and can watch some of the family activity, will make a safe environment to keep it out of trouble and provide a quiet refuge. Put plenty of newspaper on the floor and be sure the puppy's sleeping area is free from draft. A few toys of its own and a chew-proof bed will make the new quarters complete.

The bed may be a three-sided wooden box with an opening on the fourth side for entering and exiting. We do not recommend cardboard boxes and baskets, because they will be destroyed in no time and will only teach your puppy to chew on things it shouldn't.

As it grows and learns house manners, its confinement will be less and less. Putting baby gates up to block off doorways is a good method to contain an older puppy, but don't let it chew on the gate.

Toys: Puppies and even older dogs should have their own toys. Small chew toys at first, then hard rubber and flavored rawhide bones are recommended. Be careful of stuffed toys that can be ripped apart, as the pieces can be swallowed. Check "squeakie" toys to be sure the "squeaker" cannot be dislodged. Most collies love to retrieve. Throwing a hard rubber ball a few feet away and encouraging the puppy to bring it back is a great game as well as one of the first learning experiences.

When to feed: Show the puppy the water bowl and food dish but do not be surprised if it doesn't eat immediately. It is better to put the food away for awhile until the excitement has worn off a bit. Offer the puppy about half of what it normally would eat at the time you expect to feed it everyday. If it finishes the food in a few minutes, offer a little more. If this amount is not eaten, throw it away and wait until the next feeding.

Getting acquainted: Give your puppy time to become acquainted. Too much playing and holding will only confuse a young dog. At first, it may not be as playful or outgoing as it seemed to be with its littermates, but try to realize that everything is strange to it and that the safety and protection it felt in its other surroundings are no longer there. Gaining the puppy's confidence can best be done if it is treated gently and spoken to in a calm and friendly tone. Loud noises and sudden movements, grabbing at it, and teasing will only frighten the puppy.

Lifting: Do not lift your puppy by the scruff of the neck or by its front, letting the back legs dangle. Instead, teach everyone in the household to pick the puppy up by putting one hand under the chest and the other under the hindquarters. Young children should be encouraged to sit on the floor before picking up a puppy in order to keep the puppy from being dropped and perhaps suffering permanent injury. Tail pulling, squeezing, and other forms of rough play should be discouraged immediately! A live animal is *not* a plaything but can become a lifelong friend once you have won its confidence.

Sleep: Like babies, all puppies need a great deal of sleep. Keeping a schedule for eating, playtime, and sleep helps the puppy know what is to be expected and in a very short time it will know how to act accordingly. The

The proper way to hold your puppy.

first few nights, your puppy may not want to be left alone and will cry for attention. Leaving a radio on low, a clock ticking, or giving it a stuffed toy (without buttons or hair to be pulled off and swallowed) can sometimes offer comfort to a lonely puppy. Putting a warm hot water bottle wrapped in a blanket may help for the first few nights but these props should not be used for a prolonged period. Try not to go to your crying puppy more than once or twice to offer comfort; then stay only a brief time, reassuring it with a quiet and gentle voice. Leave the room immediately. The crying will eventually stop as the puppy becomes secure in its new surroundings—and peaceful nights will return.

Feeding Your Puppy

Your puppy should have its own food and water bowls. The feeding dish should be round, made of stainless steel for easy cleaning, and big enough to accommodate larger amounts of food as the puppy grows. The water bowl needs to be heavy or weighted so it cannot be pushed around or knocked over. Collie puppies like to put their paws in water to play. Keeping water in something deep enough will discourage this play and help to keep your floor from being flooded. Have fresh water available at all times, keeping it in the same place so your puppy will know where to find it.

Feeding should be done at approximately the same time every day and in the same place. If you are unable to feed your puppy on schedule, ask a neighbor or friend to help you out. Infrequent feeding or missing meals can cause nutritional imbalance and be detrimental to the puppies' overall health. Do not try to make up for a missed meal. Small puppies have small tummies and can not be expected to take in more food than their usual ration at any one time. If feeding a very young puppy is impossible for someone in the household to attend to, perhaps an older puppy or a grown collie would be more suitable.

Consistent repetition will help teach your puppy when it is time to eat. Creating good eating habits at an

Puppies grow rapidly during their first six months of life.

young age will be a pattern you will want to establish early; these habits remain with the dog the rest of its life.

How often? Puppies have their fastest growth rate during the first six months of life. For this reason good nutrition is very important, and will influence his health and well being as an adult dog. An eight-week-old puppy needs four meals a day—early morning, noon, early evening, and before bedtime. Not all of these meals will necessarily be the same size. The morning and evening meals will be the largest; the noon and late evening will be less. By the twelfth week, or at three months of age, three meals a day is usually sufficient. From six months to a year, two meals—morning and afternoon—should be offered. From that time on, most adult collies eat only once a day. Puppies demand more food as they grow but once maximum growth has been reached,

the daily intake will be less and will remain about the same.

Introducing new food: If you have been given a feeding schedule and names of food used by the breeder, it is wise to follow the same routine as closely as possible with the brands of food your puppy has been accustomed to. After a few days you may wish to change brands. Take care to introduce the new food very slowly by adding a small amount once or twice a day, adding a bit more each time until the former brand is completely replaced. Remember that a sudden change in diet may cause an upset at any age; therefore, it is important to proceed slowly. Watching the stool composition as the puppy eliminates each day will help you to determine if the new food is agreeing with it. A loose stool for more than one day indicates a need to start again with less of the new food or perhaps another brand. Do not try to save money on dog food. There are many good brands on the market that will fulfill your puppy's needs. Ask your veterinarian for advice if you are unfamiliar with a high-quality food.

Doghouses

Collies seem to enjoy cold weather but a puppy under the age of four months should not be left outside for long periods of time. If it is to live outside, it should have a draft-free, well-insulated doghouse that is raised off the ground and waterproof. There are many well-constructed houses that can be purchased from pet supply stores or lumber yards, or you can build one yourself. The house should be large enough for the dog to turn around in but small enough for its body to heat it. Filling the house with straw in the winter and tacking up a piece of burlap across the doorway will help keep out the wind. Be sure to get rid of the bedding in the spring to

avoid fleas and ticks. Shade is an important consideration in the summer. As much as dogs like the cooler weather in the fall and winter, they do not like or do well in extreme heat. Avoiding weather extremes in any season is advisable. Sleeping inside during the daytime in winter, then putting your collie out for the night is liable to make it ill. And remember—free access to fresh water is essential for a dog all the time.

Housebreaking

Whether your puppy lives inside the house with the family or is to be an outside dog, some basic training will be in order. It is never too early to begin housebreaking. In fact, this training should begin the very first day home. Collies by nature are clean dogs and will not soil their living quarters, if at all possible. Allowing the puppy to go outside frequently is necessary to complete the training

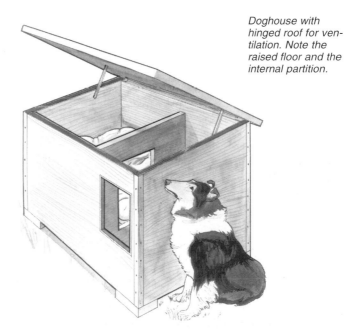

Doghouse with hinged roof for ventilation. Note the raised floor and the internal partition.

Do not forget your dog's playful nature. This sable collie is not inside a fence and may run away at any moment.

puppy will appear distracted and anxious and may whine or cry. That is the time to pick it up and carry it outside to the area you want it to use in the yard. Taking the puppy to the same place each time will allow it to get the scent of the previous time and encourage it to urinate or move its bowels. Lots of praise, a pat to say, "Good puppy," and "Good Job," expresses your pleasure, and each time it will be more eager for your approval.

A word of caution: Initially, puppies find carpet an almost irresistible target. If it should soil the carpet, blot up as much urine as possible with paper towels and use a solution of half white vinegar and half water to help eliminate the odor. Don't saturate the area; dab on some of the mixture and blot it up with a terry towel until you are satisfied the area is clean. Club soda is another effective remedy, or any good commercial cleaner with directions for removal of pet stains. Keeping the dog in the kitchen or on flooring that can be easily cleaned if an accident occurs will avoid scoldings and hurt feelings for the young dog. Of course, puppies need to be reprimanded for wrongdoings and should be told in a firm voice how displeased you are. Using the same words each time, either for praise or to scold, will tell it right away how you feel. Consistently sending the right signals teach it quickly what you expect.

Confining Your Puppy in the Yard

Having a fenced yard or a fenced play area for your puppy is an important consideration as a responsible owner, not only for the safety of your collie, but as a considerate neighbor as well. Allowing your collie to run loose only invites trouble and sometimes unfortunate accidents resulting in death. In most areas today, any dog wandering unattended and not on a

quickly. It is not uncommon for a collie puppy to be housebroken within a week if a routine is faithfully followed.

For the first several weeks or so, take the puppy outside first thing in the morning, again after it eats its breakfast, after a play session if the playtime is inside, immediately after it wakes from a nap, after every meal throughout the day, and before turning in for the night. The last outing should be as late as possible while the puppy is very young because it will not be able to control its bladder for long periods of time.

Leaving newspaper in its confined area for a few days to catch any accidents will be necessary. As it learns to use the outdoors to relieve itself, you will be able to take up the papers during the day as long as there is someone at home to take the puppy outside. When the nighttime papers remain dry, begin to take those away, too. Your puppy will try to tell you when it needs to go out by putting its nose to the floor and moving about quickly, sometimes in circles. The

leash will be picked up by the local authorities and taken to a shelter. If you are lucky enough to find your dog there, you will have to pay a hefty fine. A collie puppy is an irresistible sight and a puppy found outside alone is sure to be stolen. Dognapping is a serious problem in this country. Many dogs are stolen out of the owners' yards and transported across state lines to other communities for resale through pet stores, while others are sold for research purposes. These sad facts are not meant to frighten you as an owner but to educate and make you aware of the dangers.

Confining Your Puppy Within the House

If you leave your puppy alone in the house without being confined, you are courting disaster. All puppies chew and look for new things to play with, not knowing that your favorite table or chair leg does not belong to it. Scatter rugs, drapery hems, your most expensive shoes, or your children's video games all seem like toys to an inquisitive and investigating pup. Boredom from being alone will cause dogs to bark, creating a problem that is hard to break. Leaving your dog—puppy or grown—alone for long periods of time, is not a good idea. Collies are social animals and require people in their lives. If you must be away and there is not a family member able to check on your collie, investigate the possibility of a dog walker or a person who will come to the house a few times during the day to feed and let your dog outside for a brief period of play.

Walking on a Leash

Taking your puppy with you whenever possible acquaints it to many different situations and gives it experiences that will enable it to feel confident and calm, no matter what comes

along. Early leash training, and learning a few simple commands makes trips with you fun. Teaching a young puppy to walk on a leash takes only a few lessons. Start by putting a light collar around its neck. Make sure it is not too tight but snug enough so that the pup will not be able to slip it off or get it caught on something. It will feel strange to it at first and it will try to get it off by scratching or shaking. Distract the puppy with a toy or a game and it will soon forget all about it.

Pay particular attention to the fit of the collar. You will need to replace it several times as the dog grows. When the puppy seems comfortable wearing the collar, snap on a lightweight leash and let it drag the leash along behind it. This exercise should be done in the house, under supervision, for only a few minutes at a time. After a few days, try this outside. You must stay with the dog so that the leash does not become entangled. Now pick up the leash, letting the puppy lead you around. If it seems reluctant, get in front of it and

Puppies, like young children, should be taught lessons with patience, repetition and praise for a strong bond of love and friendship to form between them and your family.

coax it with treats. Don't forget to give it something when it begins to walk along properly. Lots of praise and petting will let your puppy know that it is doing a good thing and, before long, it will know when it sees the collar and leash in your hand that it will be going out with you and you will be greeted with excitement and anticipation.

The Car

Riding in the car should be something your collie does with ease. Learning to lie down and remain quiet while traveling is another early lesson to be taught. This can be done with two people, one working with the puppy while the other is driving. Even though the puppy is still small, it will eventually grow into a big dog. For this reason, it must be taught to ride in the back seat. If you have room, putting your dog in a wire cage is the safest way to travel. Don't be surprised if at first the puppy drools excessively or becomes upset. Taking short trips at the beginning will accustom it to the motion of the car and it should quickly learn to travel well.

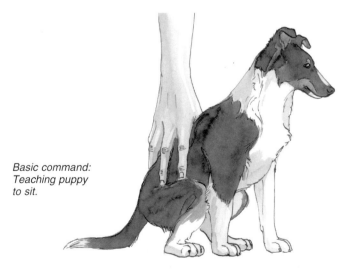

Basic command: Teaching puppy to sit.

Once your puppy has learned to walk along with you and can ride in the car, introducing it to other people and places will be an easy thing to accomplish.

Basic Commands

A few basic commands can be taught to a young puppy but it is better to wait a few months for more formalized training. The attention span of a young dog is not very long so the lessons must be short.

Coming when called: Learning its name and to come when called should be taught as soon as possible. Rewarding the puppy with a treat and praise each time it comes when its name is called makes this important lesson fun. The first few times you work with the puppy, squat down or sit on the floor. Pat the floor with your hand loud enough to get its attention and call its name in an excited tone of voice. When it looks at you, hold out your arms and continue to call its name. If the puppy doesn't come right away, get up and start to run in the opposite direction, tempting it to chase after you. As it gets closer to you, stop and praise it for being so smart. Keep this lesson a routine for several days until the puppy comes when called. Always reward your puppy when it comes to you. Never call it to you for discipline. Even when it is older, this will send mixed signals and the puppy certainly will not want to come when called and may in fact run the other way.

"Sit": Teaching your puppy to sit is a little harder but can be done over a period of time if you keep with it. This command should wait for a few weeks while your puppy matures and its attention span expands. Use the word "Sit" each time you want it to, and, at the same time, gently push its rear down until it is in the sitting position. Lots of praise and a treat when it

Puppy Training at a Glance

Eating at meal time	Offer food at the same time each day. Allow 15 or 20 minutes for the puppy to complete its meal. Throw away the uneaten portion. Learn to feed the correct amount of food by how much the puppy consumes at each meal. Keep treats to minimum, use only when training.
Sleeping	Small puppies require a lot of rest and should be given a safe place to sleep. Give reassurance for the first few nights, along with a ticking clock or radio left on low and perhaps a warm hot water bottle wrapped securely in a towel.
Come when called	Sit down and pat the floor to get puppy's attention. Call its name followed by "come." Use an excited tone of voice. Reward the puppy when it comes to you. Retrieving a ball or playing hide and seek are other games used to teach the command "come."
Sit when ordered	This command is taught after the puppy knows how to come on command. Say "sit" each time while very gently you push down on its rear. Each time puppy completes this command, praise and a treat will enforce its confidence to do it again.
Walking on leash	Use a nylon leash with a well-fitting lightweight leather collar and let the puppy drag it around the house, with supervision, for a few minutes at a time. After a few times take puppy outside and let it lead you around for the first outings. With the leash in one hand and a squeaky toy or treat in the other, coax the puppy into following you. Lots of praise will teach your puppy to look forward to trips on the leash.
Housebreaking	Taking the puppy outside to the same place each time to "potty," and a watchful eye for signs indicating that the puppy needs to go will get the training accomplished within a week or so.

obeys will tell your puppy again that it is doing something really good and it will be eager to do what you ask before very long.

By the time the puppy reaches six months of age and you have been consistent with your training, it should know how to eat at meal time, sleep quietly at night, come when its name is called, walk on the leash, ride in the car, and the meaning of the word "No." Excessive barking, jumping up on people, rough play, such as hand-biting or pulling on trouser legs, should have been discouraged.

Your collie should know the difference between your belongings and its toys. It is still a young dog and will continue to do puppy things, but by now it understands when you are pleased and when it has done something wrong.

Visiting the Veterinarian

One of the first trips you take with your puppy should be to the veterinarian. He or she will give your new puppy a thorough examination and put it on a schedule for a series of puppy shots and rabies inoculations.

21

Quick Reference Chart for Canine Infectious Diseases

Sign or Symptom	Canine Distemper	Infectious Canine Hepatitis	Parvoviral Gastroenteritis	Coronaviral Gastroenteritis	Para-influenza	Leptospirosis	Rabies
Vomiting	X	X	X	X		X	
Diarrhea	X	X	X*	X**		X	
"Cold" or "flu"	X	†		X	X	†	
Convulsions, seizures, "fits"	X	†				†	X
Hardening of the foot and nose pads	X						

*The diarrhea seen in cases of parvoviral gastroenteritis often is light-gray, yellow-gray, or hemorrhagic.
**The diarrhea seen in coronaviral gastroenteritis often is yellow-orange, occasionally bloody.
†A variable sign in this disease.
(From Fredric L. Frye's *Mutts.* Barron's: New York, 1989. Reprinted with permission.)

The common diseases against which young puppies are routinely immunized are canine distemper, infectious canine hepatitis, canine parvoviral gastroen- teritis, canine coronaviral gastroenteri- tis, parainfluenza, leptospirosis, and rabies. Polyvalent vaccines that contain the immunizing agents for the first six diseases are available, so your dog will have to receive only one broad-scope injection plus another for rabies vacci- nation. This immunization is repeated at eight, twelve, and sixteen weeks of age. Rabies immunization is given at four months of age. From then on annual checkups and booster shots are all that will be necessary unless, of course, your collie becomes ill or injured.

It is important to stay on the sched- ule your veterinarian gives you. He or she is vaccinating your puppy against diseases that are life-threatening and providing protection that the puppy's immune system cannot handle.

However, due to misinformation or a simple mistake your dog may become infected. The above chart will help you to recognize the disease.

An early visit to the veterinarian is a must. Never post- pone a required vaccination.

If the seller has given you a health record, be sure to take it with you. Depending upon the age of your puppy, it may have already had some of its shots and your veterinarian will need this information. This is also a good time to ask questions about diet, diet supplements, and general health care. Be sure to ask about heart worm preventatives and how to control fleas and ticks.

When you call to make an appointment, the receptionist will probably ask you to bring a stool sample to be tested for parasites, commonly called worms. Try to collect as fresh a sample as possible. Using a plastic bag on your hand is an easy way to pick up a small amount of feces. Deposit it in a small clean container, like a baby food jar, cover it with plastic wrap, and attach a label with the dog's name and the date.

Whether or not you have purchased your puppy on a spay or neutering contract, your first visit to the veterinarian is a good time to discuss these procedures. The need to control pet overpopulation caused by indiscriminate breeding is an important consideration and one you must address. Aside from the population issue, there are many benefits associated with early spaying or neutering. Decreasing the incidence of mammary and testicular tumors, of which an alarming number have been found to be cancerous, is just one of the benefits.

If you don't know a veterinarian, before you bring your new puppy home, check with friends who already own dogs for recommendations or call local breeders for suggestions. Choosing one that is close to your home is helpful, but should not be the only determining factor. The office should be clean and free from odors. The doctor and staff should be friendly and polite, ready to answer questions freely and to discuss treatments in an easy-to-understand manner. Do not hesitate to ask about fees and methods of payment, but shopping price is not a particularly good idea and usually the costs are about the same in a given area. Of course you should know ahead of time what to expect. Also ask about emergency hours. For some reason, most critical problems arise after office hours, on holidays or weekends.

Most males and females get along together regardless of whether they are of the same sex or not. Two or more dogs living in the same household should definitely be spayed or neutered.

Growing Up

For most children, a collie puppy proves more exciting than any other form of entertainment or gift. A furry puppy dashing around the house creates an atmosphere of delight for the whole family.

Grooming Your Collie

The collie coat is described as its "crowning glory"; therefore, proper care from the dog's owner is not only beneficial but necessary. Grooming your collie is easier than perhaps it may first appear. A thorough brushing once a week takes care of the thickest coat and encourages the natural oils to repel odor, dirt, and matting.

A few correct grooming tools make the job easier. Most commonly used is the pin brush, a wood or plastic long-handled brush with stainless steel pins that will get through the densest coat. Be sure the pins are not so stiff as to break the hair. A pair of small sharp scissors, a metal comb, nail cutters, and a plastic spray bottle will help you keep your collie looking and feeling good.

Elevating your dog on a sturdy table, preferably a grooming table available at pet supply outlets, will help you perform the grooming. The dog should learn at a young age to stand quietly on the table, enabling you to walk around it easily for a complete examination. In summer, a daily exam for ticks and fleas is especially important. If they are present, see your veterinarian.

Check the inside of its ears: Excess dirt or wax should be carefully wiped away by using a little warm water, rubbing alcohol, or an ear cleaning solution made for dogs. Dab lightly around the inside with a cotton ball. If no problem is apparent, cleaning need be done only on a monthly basis.

The eyes should be bright and clear without any discharge. Any matter in or around the eyes should be gently wiped away with warm water. Start at the inside corner and work out. The appearance of pus or excessive discharge indicates a probable infection and a call to the veterinarian is in order.

A look inside the mouth for tooth tartar buildup or dental problems is recommended. This examination is important for a puppy, too, especially when baby teeth are loosening and permanent teeth are beginning to come in. Watch for correct alignment to ensure proper chewing. Offering your collie hard bones such as (Milk Bones®) and rawhide chew bones help to keep the teeth clean. It is now widely accepted that regularly brushing the dog's teeth with a tooth paste or dental solution especially manufactured for dogs has proved effective against gum problems and the accumulation of plaque.

The feet and nails should be trimmed about once a month. Using a nail clipper for the first time can be a frightening experience for you and your collie. Ask your veterinarian or a professional groomer to show you how to use the clippers. This part of the grooming ritual is probably the hardest part for most people. Dogs don't particularly like to have their feet fussed with, so learning the correct way from the beginning will save time and keep you and your collie happier. Occasionally, you might cut a toenail too short and it will start to bleed. Sometimes it looks as though it will never stop. If you do not have a styptic pencil or quick stick such as men use for shaving cuts, push a bit of flour or cornstarch against the cut nail to help absorb and stop the bleeding. Putting pressure on the foot to walk may start the bleeding again. Have your dog lie down for a few minutes and everything will soon be back to normal. You will feel terrible but don't worry—after a soothing apology, your collie will readily forgive you. Clipping the nails and keeping them short allows the dog to walk more comfortably. Cutting the hair around the pads on the bottom of the feet keeps mud and snow from caking between the toes and again adds comfort in walking.

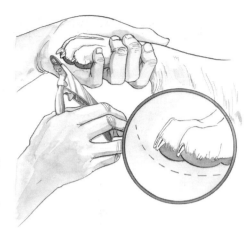

How to clip the nails of your collie.

The next item to check is matting in the coat. This happens most commonly in the soft, silky hair behind the ears, in the front leg feathering, and

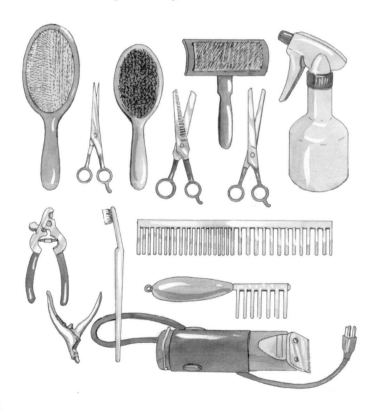

A complete selection of grooming tools for your pet.

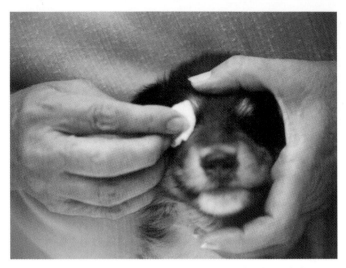

Eyes should always be bright and clear.

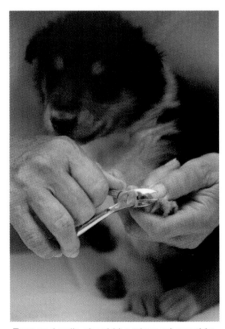

Feet and nails should be trimmed monthly.

sometimes in the thick fur on the hindquarters and rear legs. This area is often referred to as the "skirts." The best way to remove a mat is to carefully cut it away, then comb through the area to be sure that no tangles remain. Sometimes rubbing a bit of baby powder into the mat and gently working the area with your fingers and a comb will loosen it enough for you to thoroughly comb it out.

Bathing: Bathing a collie two or three times a year is usually adequate to maintain its coat. If you are exhibiting at dog shows or other events, more frequent washing will be necessary, but for general maintenance, unless something unusual occurs, occasional bathing and weekly brushing will be enough. Because of the breed's double coat—soft, close fur next to the skin with harsher and longer hair on top—it is important to use enough warm water to get the hair wet to the skin. Using a mild dog shampoo, lather the coat from the skin outward, being careful not to get soap in the eyes or ears. Rinsing shampoo from the hair is as important as the washing. Leaving soap residue in the coat or on the skin will make the hair dull and cause the skin to be dry and itchy. Towel dry the dog, then let it shake as much water as possible from it, and towel dry again. Follow by gently brushing all over to keep mats from forming.

Bathing on a warm day will allow your collie to dry naturally without becoming chilled. In cool or cold weather, keep it inside until dry. Using a hair dryer turned on the warm setting will help dry the dog more quickly. Most dogs do not appreciate this time-saving device, so towel off as much as you can. Pay special attention to the chest area, around the neck and head, and the underbelly. Keep the dog away from drafts until it is completely dry.

The rough collie's coat is its crowning glory.

The double coat of this breed requires using plenty of water at bath time.

the bottle used for misting plants) filled with water to mist the whole coat. Take your pin brush and begin just behind the ears, brushing the hair forward. Using this method will enable the natural oils in the hair follicles to be brought to the hairtips, giving the coat a shiny appearance when you are finished. As you spray and brush, the coat will stand up. After brushing the whole coat in this manner, gently brush the hair in a downward motion. The coat will now appear in its natural state. Don't forget the chest and tail. If the white parts or feet and legs are a bit dull, mist the area and rub cornstarch or baby powder into and against the hair. Let this dry while brushing the rest of the dog. Finally, when the white parts of the coat are dry, brush these areas with short, upward strokes, removing the excess powder.

When you have completed the grooming, carefully take your collie off the table, and let it have a good shake to arrange the hair. Its beauty will be your reward.

Training

Collies are by instinct herding dogs—they want to work, to have a job. As they grow older, their sense of pleasing their owner and trying to anticipate his or her wishes or moods becomes very evident. Even though their herding ability and eagerness to take on responsibilities around the home seem a natural part of their makeup, this eagerness does not always carry over into formalized obedience training. Collies take harsh correction very personally. They don't have to be told many times that they have done or are doing something displeasing to you. Hitting a collie with your hand, or worse with a rolled-up newspaper, in order to punish it for a misdeed, will only give you an unhappy and reluctant dog. The collie's natural sweet and gentle nature seem to

Shedding: Shedding in both the rough- and smooth-coated collie occurs once or twice a year. Males usually shed within two or three months after their birthday. Females tend to shed shortly after the end of their season if they have not been spayed. When the hair is noticeably loose, you will see the undercoat loosening or coming out as you brush, in which case a warm bath is in order. A daily brushing and combing will help complete this cycle and encourage new coat growth. Shedding will take about three weeks, and approximately six to ten weeks for the new coat replacement. The collie coat protects against heat as well as cold and should not be cut or shaved except for medical reasons.

Brushing your collie on a weekly basis can be done easily and quickly after you have practiced a few times. Use a plastic spray bottle (similar to

make it almost impossible for it to understand or accept, angry and imprudent conduct. While they are quick to forgive your anger, they will not respond to your training with the happiness and eagerness you would like to see. This does not mean, however, that firmness and reprimands are not in order while teaching your dog the things you want it to do. Once the lesson has been learned, lavish praise and a hug will imprint the message in a way that will be rewarding to you both.

Like all dogs, collies are also pack animals. Their heritage dictates there must be leaders and followers. All it has learned as an infant puppy, it learned from its dam. Now that it is in your care, it must learn that you are the leader. Rarely does a collie challenge authority of a human being. The exceptions would of course include imminent danger to its family and, in some cases, threats to its territory. Establishing yourself as a pack leader, or Alpha, is an important step early in the dog's training.

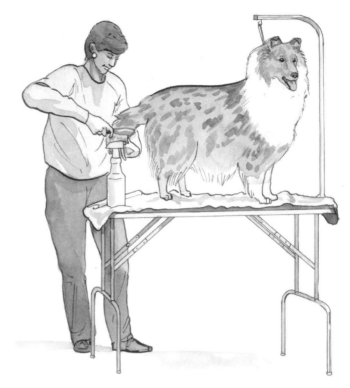

When to Begin

Other than some very basic training referred to earlier, obedience training should begin at about six months of age. If, after a few lessons, you see that the dog is reluctant or unhappy about continuing them, it might be wise to put them off for a while.

The primary reason for early obedience training is to ensure a manageable big dog. While it is still young and small and can be picked up, you have to remember that it will some day weigh between 70 and 80 or more pounds—a dog you will want to control with voice commands and trust that it will obey. Obedience training not only gives you a well-behaved collie, but adds a measure of self-confidence to the dog. A well-trained dog is ready for all kinds of work around the home as well as in the community or, should

you choose, competition at dog events earning degrees and titles, including the coveted title Obedience Champion.

The Importance of Exercise

An important factor in the health and well-being of your collie is exercise. A dog that has exercise on a daily basis will have less pent-up energy that can lead to misbehavior.

You should be part of your dog's exercise program, overseeing play or acting as a partner while walking or on an outing. The benefits you and your dog should reap if both form a team engaged in daily physical activity are many. Not only will both become healthier, but you also will strengthen a growing emotional bond that will last throughout the years.

A professional grooming table reduces stress and the amount of time it takes to get top results.

29

A partnership with mutual benefits.

want to keep an eye on the play to be sure one is not so dominant over the other as to cause a threat of safety.

Collies love a good romp in the snow, leaping in and out of snow drifts, using their nose to toss the powdery stuff into the air. Collies very often do not like to be out in the rain, and swimming is not a favorite pastime either. The added weight of a wet coat makes swimming difficult.

When dogs are left alone all day, it is doubly important that they have a routine exercise program. Routine is the key word here—dogs of all ages thrive on routine. Physical and mental exercise keep the body and mind busy. Keeping up with your dog's learned obedience commands is an excellent way to challenge its mind. Ask it to "Sit" before it eats or is given a treat, when you attach the leash, or before you throw a ball. Vary the situations with the "Down, stay" command. Call the dog to you using its name several times throughout the play period, and use the "Heel" command when walking or running.

Very young puppies should not be encouraged to take long jogging runs or to jump. Putting too much stress on growing and developing bodies can cause serious injuries and malformation of shoulders, hips, and legs.

Exercise and strenuous activities should be curtailed in very hot or humid weather; try to get out with your dog very early in the morning, even before the sun is up, for a walk or a game of chase and fetch. In this day of fitness awareness, a two- or three-mile walk with your collie should be just the thing to get your day off to a good start.

A collie will play for a long time chasing after a ball or stick, happily returning it to you for another chance to run for it. Some have become quite proficient with a Frisbee as well. Putting your dog out in the backyard by itself is not exercise unless there is another dog to play with. Even then, you will

A wonderful rough blue merle collie.

Grooming finished, your dog's beauty will be your reward.

A beautiful rough tricolor specimen.

One, the collie is born with a strong herding instinct. Two, it is a pack animal. Knowing that they respond easily to assigned tasks and that you must be the leader will prove helpful during the dog's training.

It can also be helpful to hire a dog walker to come in the middle of the day to exercise the dog. Be sure the person is reliable and will come at approximately the same time every day. This short break in the day does not take the place of a morning exercise program or an evening jaunt but should be considered an addition to other activities.

When we call our collies in for the night, one dog has taken it upon himself to make sure that all are accounted for. Normally, he is the first one to come to the door, then turns to wait for the rest to appear. If one or more have stopped along the way, for whatever reason, he will return to the runs or paddock and round up the late comer. Only when all have arrived, is he content to go into his bed. Giving us a look that tells us he is pleased with himself and his self-appointed task, he settles down for his rest.

HOW-TO:
Teaching Basic Obedience

Classes

Drawing 1

An organized training class is usually the most satisfactory method used for obedience training. The instructors are professional trainers and deal with all kinds of dogs and dog-related problems. These classes are divided into beginners, intermediate, and advanced lessons. Joining a group of people and their dogs for an hour or so once a week can be as enjoyable for the owners as for the dogs. Don't be shy about enrolling in these classes; many new and lasting friendships are made with people you may never have met under other circumstances. There is a fee for the classes and they last about ten weeks or more. You will be expected to practice the lessons at home for a period of time each day between sessions. Call kennels or dog clubs in your area for the information you need to locate instructors and the schedule of instructions. Be sure your instructor has assisted in training collies and is familiar with their temperament, as each breed is different in the way they take to formalized instruction. If you are not satisfied with the teaching approach, ask for other recommendations. Check the yellow pages and the newspaper classified section in the Sunday newspaper. Sometimes obedience classes are taught at local schools and community colleges.

Obedience training provides a beginning requirement that will allow you and your collie to have many new experiences. For example, visiting hospitals, nursing homes, and schools for handicapped children, with a group or alone, is one of the most rewarding activities in which you can participate (see pages 53 to 56 for information on assistance and therapeutic collies).

Agility and herding classes

Ask your instructor about the American Kennel Club Good Citizen test and about training in agility classes. The latter are classes in which the dogs are taught to climb up, over, and through a series of obstacles in a prescribed amount of time. The dogs love these games and seem eager to master the challenge.

As you begin to network with your dog, keep your ears open for instinct herding tests to determine whether you would like to go on with training your collie to herd and earn titles at herding events held around the country. The opportunities are there for you and your collie to take part in many activities and programs or to just enjoy hours of each other's company. Whichever way you choose, your collie will also enjoy having a good companion.

1. Professional training ensures satisfactory results.

2. Receiving the command "Heel."

Training at Home

Training your collie at home on an informal basis can also be effective. Teaching the basic commands of "Sit," "Down," "Stay," and "Heel" may be taught without any formal training when you are consistent in your methods and with your time. If your puppy can sit on command, come when it is called, and respond appropriately to the word "No," you are well on your way. Getting its attention and keeping eye contact is very important. Creating a pleasant learning atmosphere while remaining serious during training lets the dog know that this is not playtime but something you want it to do when asked.

Be sure to use the same words each time for the commands you are teaching. Teach the other members in the household which words you are using for commands. For example, telling the dog to "Sit" one time and saying "Down" the next, expecting it to sit, will

obviously confuse the dog. There are books and manuals in the library, bookstore, or pet supply outlet to help you learn these commands and methods.

"Heel"
Drawing 2
After your collie has reached the age of six months and is able to sit on command and walk along on the leash, the command "Heel" is the next lesson. Heeling keeps the dog walking along beside you, close to your left leg, without pulling on the leash.
Drawing 3
The "Heel" command requires the use of a stainless steel chain collar, referred to as a choke chain. They come in various lengths, but should not be more than four inches longer than the fit around the dog's neck. There is a ring on both ends of the collar. When putting this collar on your dog, you must first double part of the chain through one of the rings

3. Choke chain on smooth-coated collie.

to form a sort of noose. As you face your dog, slip the chain over its head so that the top of the chain connected to the free ring is resting on top of the neck, not underneath the chin. Snap a leather leash on the free ring. As you pull up on the leash the collar should close quickly and release again as pressure is released. Be sure the chain is on the dog correctly or it will not release smoothly and could cause the dog to choke. This type of collar is designed for two purposes—it combines comfort for the dog, assuming it fits properly, and offers control for the handler.

To begin the lesson, your collie should be in the sitting position on your left side looking straight ahead. Place the end of the leash in your right hand and pass the rest of it across your body, holding the remainder in your left hand a few inches above his neck. Your left hand will be used to supply the corrective action. As you step off on your left foot, give a slight upward jerk on the leash and the command "Heel." As the dog begins to move out in front of you, give another quick jerking motion using the word "Heel" again. Keep your voice firm and repeat this exercise as often as needed until your collie is walking beside you without exerting pressure on the leash. When you come to a stop, tell your dog to "Sit." Remember to release the pressure quickly as the commands are obeyed and say "Good Dog" as it begins to learn this lesson. As always, give a lot of praise when the session has ended. Training is like a game for your dog. It will be eager to please you but is likely to become bored if it goes on too long. Two or three five-minute lessons will be enough for a few days; then you can expand it into two ten-minute lessons. End each lesson with some playtime after removing the choke collar and leash.

"Down"
Drawing 4

When the "Heel" command has been learned and is working well, you can proceed to another command—"Down."

As a rule, dogs are not comfortable sitting for long periods of time. Therefore, the command "Down," meaning to lie down, is a good lesson to teach. It is especially useful when traveling or visiting in a place where the dog must remain quiet. The easiest way to get the dog down is to first have it in a sitting position.

5. The "Stay" command is the last of the basic orders.

While pulling the leash in a downward motion with your right hand, push firmly on its back at about the shoulder level, giving the command "Down." It should go into the correct position. Praise it loudly.

Another method is to put the dog in the sitting position at your side. Get down on one knee with your left hand against the dog's shoulder. Using your right hand, pick the dog's left foot off the ground, while pressure from your left hand forces the dog down sideways. Do this at the same time you are saying "Down." Or, you may have the dog sit while you gently slide its front feet forward until it is in the down position. Again, issue the command in a firm voice— "Down." However you accomplish this task, praising your dog each time it completes the procedure is the reward it will be expecting. Remember not to work more than a few minutes at first, expanding the lesson time only after several sessions.

"Stay"
Drawing 5

An important command to teach your collie is "Stay." This can be done after you feel secure that your dog has mastered the "Sit" and "Down" lessons. While it is in one of these positions, hold the leash in your right hand and move a few feet away, at the same time telling it to "Sit," "Stay," or "Down," "Stay." When it begins to move or starts to get up, return to it quickly and start again with "Sit" or "Down," and then repeating "Stay" while moving away. This exercise will

4. Understanding the "Down" command.

take more time for the dog to learn, but as it begins to stay in place for a few seconds more each time, you can move farther away until you are at the end of the leash.

Teaching your collie to perform all of the above lessons with the leash off can only be accomplished with time and patience. The positive results of your training will be rewarding to you and you will have taught your dog manners to last its lifetime.

Regardless of breed, all puppies like playmates.

Health

When to Call the Veterinarian

Common sense is your best guide to evaluating your collie's health. When you notice a deviation in its usual daily patterns, take a few minutes to determine whether or not there is a problem.

Diarrhea: The most common symptom you will notice is diarrhea. All dogs have occasionally loose stools. Usually it is due to a change in diet or, at the very least, something it has eaten that does not agree with it. If the condition becomes acute and frequent, if the stool is passed as liquid, or if you see blood, call the veterinarian.

Loss of appetite: If the dog is normally a good eater and its appetite goes off for a couple of days, it should be examined for an abscessed tooth, or for internal problems.

Ears: Excess scratching or digging around its ears, holding its head to one side, or shaking its head from time to time indicates a possible ear infection and will need the attention of the veterinarian.

Choking: Choking or difficulty in swallowing are obvious symptoms of a problem in the throat. Pry apart the jaws and look in the mouth for any foreign objects. If you find nothing there, an appointment with the veterinarian for further evaluation is necessary. Persistent coughing can be due to diseases of the throat and respiratory system or to parasites and should be investigated.

Coat: If you notice that your collie's coat is not as shiny as usual, perhaps thinning and dry, if its skin appears flaky and it is losing weight, consult your veterinarian who will do a fecal examination for internal parasites. This should be a routine examination every six months or so anyway, just to avoid such problems. Specific patches of hair loss, exposing red or inflamed skin, may indicate mange. This can be treated by your veterinarian with dips and prescription ointments.

Other signs: Obvious signs such as prolonged limping, vomiting, fever, excessive intake of water, frequent urination, or wincing in pain when touched are all reasons to call the veterinarian. Collies are almost always stoic, rarely whimpering or crying out when in pain. For this reason, it is all the more important to be alert to changes in behavior and overall health.

In case of an emergency, it is a good idea to keep an emergency telephone number close at hand for weekends and after office hours.

Collies are normally strong, healthy animals. They live to be 12 or 13 years old with relatively few problems. But like all living creatures, they are subject to diseases and birth defects.

Fortunately, the number of genetic health-related problems found in collies are few. A genetic or inherited problem most associated with them is that of the collie eye anomaly (see page 83). This condition may be diagnosed as early as six weeks of age and does not vary in severity as the dog matures. The defect, if slight, does not seem to affect vision, but it is a problem you should discuss with the breeder. All collie puppies should have their eyes examined by a qualified canine ophthalmologist before

Jumping up on you is a form of greeting. Don't discourage the greeting, but teach your dog other ways of showing affection. Stoop down and guide its feet away from you while petting and talking to your puppy. This is easier than having a 60- or 70-pound dog put its muddy paws all over your best clothes. Ask family members and friends to greet your puppy in the same way.

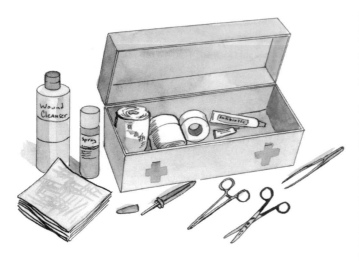

Sooner or later you will need a first-aid kit (therefore, have one ready now).

day or so afterwards until it may suddenly begin to hemorrhage. Therefore, no matter how minor you feel the emergency is, it is always best to follow the incident with a visit to the veterinarian for a thorough examination.

Using common sense is the best way to deal with an emergency. While a knowledge of first aid is important for you and your collie, not having to put this knowledge to the test is far more gratifying. As in all medical situations requiring fast action, the cardinal rule is not to panic but to remain calm and think about what you are doing. If there is time, call someone for assistance—the adage that two heads are better than one is often true. Keeping your dog safe from harm is as much your duty as it is the dog's to protect you—and never leave your dog in someone else's care without providing emergency phone numbers for your veterinarian as well as yourself.

First aid kit: It is helpful to have a box or container of some kind in which to keep emergency supplies handy. You should gather these supplies not long after your new collie comes to live with you. Be sure to label the container carefully and keep track of the contents so that medications with expiration dates are kept updated. Some of the items you will need are:

- Rectal thermometer
- 3 × 3 inch (7.6 cm) and 4 × 4 inch sterile gauze pads
- gauze bandage, 2 inch and 3 inch (7.6 cm) sizes
- self-adhesive bandage roll
- cotton pads, balls, and swabs
- adhesive tape
- hydrogen peroxide for cleansing wounds
- antiseptic for minor cuts
- germicidal soap
- antibacterial skin cream
- blunt-tipped scissors
- antidiarrhea preparation, such as Kaopectate®.

purchase. A proper examination cannot be done by a veterinarian with a flashlight.

Progressive retinal atrophy, commonly referred to as PRA (see page 84), is a disease of the retina and will cause blindness. Have the dog tested at six months if you have reason to believe the condition exists and the dog does not see well.

While such conditions as cancer, bloat, and immune system problems are known to occur in the breed, it is still unknown if these conditions are hereditary and which could be the causes.

Hip displasia is rarely found in collies.

First Aid

In the case of an accident, a knowledge of first aid may help to save your dog's life. Accidents happen at unexpected times and it is not always possible to reach your veterinarian in an emergency. However, it is important to recognize your own limitations. Your quick action could help your dog before you get help but it may have suffered extensive internal injuries (from a fall or from being struck by a car) and not show any signs of it for a

Ask your veterinarian for other suggestions or comments as to what items to keep on hand.

Temperature: The normal temperature for an adult dog is 100° to 103°F. The average is 101.3°F (38.3°C).

The only effective way to take your dog's temperature is with a rectal thermometer. Shake down the thermometer until the bulb registers 96°F (35.5°C). Lubricate the bulb with Vaseline. Raise your dog's tail, holding it firmly to keep the dog from sitting down, and gently insert the bulb into the anal canal with a twisting motion, about two inches. Keep the thermometer in place about three minutes. Remove it, wipe it clean, and read the temperature as indicated by the height of the mercury column against the numbered scale.

Clean the thermometer with alcohol before putting it away and before using it again. This will prevent the transfer of diseases.

The normal pulse is 70 to 130 beats per minute at rest. Normal respiration is 10 to 30 breaths per minute at rest.

Internal bleeding: Internal injuries are not always apparent after an accident, but if the gums are pale gray in color and the dog is weak or prostrate, it may be hemorrhaging internally. Using an improvised stretcher made from a door or a couple of large flat boards fastened together is by far the best method of transporting an injured dog. If neither of these is available to you, use a blanket or large coat, tying knots in each corner. Place strong poles through the knots so that two people can carry the dog to the car. Try not to change the dog's position when sliding it onto a stretcher. Take it to the nearest veterinary clinic; time is *not* on your side.

Bleeding from the nose but no apparent damage to the nostrils may indicate a head injury. If there is bleeding from the mouth, inspect the

tongue and inside the mouth for cuts. Even when there is no immediate sign of internal bleeding, an examination after an accident is strongly recommended.

Choking: The sound of a dog choking should bring you to its aid immediately—it may have something caught in its throat. Open the mouth wide by placing one hand on the lower jaw and one hand around the top of the muzzle. Then pry open the jaws and take a look. If you cannot see anything, push your finger into the throat as deeply as possible and rub the surface gently to try and dislodge any small obstruction that might be present. If you cannot determine the cause of the choking, call for veterinarian assistance.

Occasionally, food or a bone can become lodged crosswise in the back of the mouth behind the teeth or between the teeth and outer gums. The dog will open and close its mouth, shake its head, or lower its head and try to get its foot into its mouth to dislodge the cause of the discomfort.

A stretcher can be easily improvised using household items.

All senior citizens deserve special consideration, and the rule applies to dogs as well.

can splinter a cooked bone in just a few minutes. The splinters then become lodged in the throat or, worse, in the intestine. Once in the intestine, the small sharp pieces of bone can perforate or puncture the intestine wall. Often, a very expensive surgical procedure will be needed to remove the bone fragment—all this because you thought you were doing a nice thing for your collie! To save the dog a great deal of pain and discomfort, and to save you an unnecessary and expensive trip to the veterinarian, make it a hard and fast rule not to give your dog *any* type of meat bone. The only exception might be a raw knucklebone sometimes available in a butcher shop or at grocery store meat counters. Today, there are plenty of good bone substitutes found in the pet supply stores. A good rawhide bone, knotted at both ends, will offer many hours of chewing and will keep your collie satisfied and occupied.

Eyes: Cuts and scratches may cause a mild inflammation in your dog's eyes. Use an eye lotion especially made for dogs or a solution of boric acid to gently wash the eye. If neither is available, use warm tap water. Dry the area with sterile gauze or a clean, lint-free, soft cloth. An accumulation of pus under the upper or lower eyelids or swollen lids, may indicate conjunctivitis, or the beginning of an infection. Discharge from the eye or noticeable hair loss around the rim are other signs of trouble to watch for. Aside from cleaning the area as described above, consult your veterinarian who will determine the treatment. Important: Administering salves or ointments without knowing the specific cause of the problem could cause irreparable damage.

Cuts: Most cuts are not severe. Allowing your collie to clean the wound by licking the area with its tongue will help to promote healing. The saliva

Usually it is a simple matter to remove the article but it may require two people to get the job done—one to hold the dog's mouth open and the other to grab the object with the fingers and get it loose. If this approach is unsuccessful, take your collie to the veterinarian immediately.

Persistent vomiting is an unmistakable symptom of something lodged in the intestinal tract, indicating that the object has gone past the throat. A veterinarian must be the one to decide the method of treatment.

Very often, people think they are giving their dog a wonderful treat by giving the dog a steak bone or some other type of meat bone. Collies, like most dogs have very strong jaws and

40

secreted from the mouth contains beneficial enzymes.

Clean the cut with hydrogen peroxide to kill bacteria and help prevent infection. Clip away the hair to allow the affected area to remain free of matting and to keep hair from getting caught in the wound. Air circulation is necessary to healing as well and is especially important if the wound is on the neck or shoulder area. Keep the area as clean as possible and watch for any sign of infection. A check with the veterinarian for some antibiotic salve will sometimes speed up the healing process. Remember that your dog will probably want to lick the ointment off if it is in an area it can reach so try to keep the dog interested in something else while the medication is penetrating the area.

A jagged cut or tear that appears deep, or a puncture wound, should be seen by a veterinarian as soon as possible. Both will need to be checked for foreign matter and will no doubt need antibiotic treatment. In the case of an elongated tear or laceration that is unusually deep, stitches will be needed to close the area. Until you can get the dog to the veterinarian, cut the hair away as close to the skin as possible and administer hydrogen peroxide to the wound. If the wound is on the face or legs, place a sterile gauze pad over the site and try to close or keep the area from widening by placing two Band-Aids® or adhesive tape in the form of an "X" on top of the gauze pad and attaching it to healthy skin. This probably will not hold very long because of the hair, but it is worth a try. Keep the dog quiet until you receive professional help.

Severe arterial bleeding: Blood from a severed artery will be bright red and flow in spurts, in time to the heartbeat. The blood from a cut vein is darker red and will flow evenly. To stop the bleeding from an artery, apply

pressure between the heart and wound so that as little blood as possible can run out. To stop the bleeding from a cut, apply pressure below the wound. Use a piece of bedsheet, a cotton undershirt, or a nylon stocking as a tourniquet. Place it in the correct position for the type of wound and twist the ends together until the right amount of pressure has been applied to control the bleeding. Remember to release the pressure every ten minutes or so. When the bleeding has been controlled, wash the area with clean water and a soft cloth and cover it with sterile gauze, then with cotton (don't place the cotton directly over the injury), and wrap with a bandage.

The average life span of a collie is about 11 to 13 years.

41

Be careful not to bandage so tightly as to stop the circulation. Take the collie to your veterinarian promptly, keeping it as quiet as possible while traveling. If someone cannot drive you to the veterinarian, put the dog in a crate to keep it from moving about and reopening the wound.

Shock: The most common forms of shock are caused by heatstroke, burns, or being hit by a car; however, shock may occur after any injury. The dog may be in a state of complete collapse or unusually nervous excitement. The symptoms are a weak pulse and shallow breathing. The eyes appear "glassy" and the gums are usually pale—signs of impending circulation failure. Keep the dog as quiet as possible. Keep loud noises and talk to a minimum so that it will not try to move. If the weather is cool, cover the dog with a coat or warm blanket. Try to keep its body warm and at an even temperature.

Heatstroke: Heatstroke occurs when the dog is left exposed to severe heat from the sun and humidity or when left in a parked car or small building where there is insufficient air circulation. Many dogs are found dead every summer, left in parked cars while the owner runs into the store "for just a minute." On an average summer day in a closed car, the temperature can reach an unbearable 160°. Your collie could die within fifteen minutes even with your car windows partly open, or its heart and lungs could be permanently damaged by excessive heat or humidity. Leave your dog at home in the summer where it will have plenty of shade and fresh water. If you leave your dog in your backyard, be sure there is a shaded area to protect it.

In the case of heatstroke, a dog's temperature is elevated to a dangerous level and its body must be cooled as quickly as possible. Move the dog into the shade if it is outside. Apply ice packs or immerse it in cool water. If neither of these methods is available, use the garden hose to wet it down. Keep the dog as quiet as possible. You should see some improvement in a few minutes. Take it to your veterinarian as soon as possible in case additional treatment is necessary. The dog may need oxygen therapy or intravenous injected fluids.

Burns: In all cases of burn accidents, try to cut the hair away as close to the skin as possible before treatment. For a small burn caused by fire or heat, a pain-killing household burn ointment may be used. If the burn is caused by an acid, wash the area with warm tap water and apply a solution of baking soda. If your dog was scalded by boiling water, immediately douse liberally with cold water and apply ice for a few minutes. If the burn was caused by a caustic agent, use vinegar to treat the surface area. Keep the burned areas as clean as possible until you can get further professional help for any burn more severe than a small spot.

Drowning: All dogs can swim but even the strongest swimmer can drown if it becomes exhausted. Because the rough collie carries such a thick and heavy coat, it is at a great disadvantage in the water. Once the hair becomes water-logged, it acts as an additional weight. The collie will tire quickly and may need help getting to shore or to dry ground. Your collie should not be encouraged to swim in a pool. If it should accidentally fall into a steep-sided swimming pool or pond, there is very little place for it to get a good foothold or find an area where it can get out.

Should your collie get itself into this situation and you need to revive it, the remedy is much like that given to a human being. Before giving artificial respiration, hold your dog up by the hindlegs at the hocks (the area where the upper and lower leg meets) to expel the excess water out of the lungs. Lay the dog on a flat surface with the right side down, extend the head and neck, and pull the tongue forward. Then push down on the ribcage, releasing the pressure rhythmically every four or five seconds. Another method to use is "mouth-to-nose" respiration. Pull the tongue forward and close the mouth. Seal the lips with your hand. Place your mouth over the dog's nose and blow in steadily for three seconds. The chest will expand. Release to let the air come back out. Keep this up with regularity. As long as there is a heartbeat, there is hope. When your dog begins to show signs of recovery, rub it briskly all over with a towel, then wrap it in a coat or blanket to keep it warm while taking it to the veterinarian for further treatment. This experience has caused severe stress on the dog's respiratory system and you will need professional advice on how to take care of it.

Poisoning: All household and garden products that carry the warning "Keep out of the reach of children" should also be kept away from and out of the reach of your dog. Read labels carefully when using any type of insecticides or products used to kill grasses or weeds. These types of agents can be absorbed into a dog's system through the pads on the feet. Puppies will investigate anything and older dogs may take a liking to a toxic substance such as lethal antifreeze. Prevention is better than emergency treatment and antidotes. Recognizable symptoms of poisoning are retching and heavy strings of saliva, pain, trembling, staggering, and sometimes convulsions. If you know what your dog has ingested, take a sample to your veterinarian so that he or she can administer the proper antidote. Home remedies are dangerous unless you know exactly what has caused this toxic reaction. Most universities or colleges with a veterinary school have poison control centers and are glad to answer your call for help. Again, it is important to correctly identify the cause of the poisoning.

Administering Medicine

If your veterinarian prescribes an oral medication you should know how to administer it yourself.

Liquids: Use the lip pocket method to give liquids to a dog that cannot drink from a dish or that must be forced to take liquid medicine. Hold the dog's head up. Put your fingers in the side of the mouth at the corner, and pull out the lower lip to form a pocket. Then pour or spoon the liquid into this pocket, keeping the dog's head up. The liquid will run between the teeth and down the throat so that it swallows it. Plastic vials in which pills are dispensed by the druggist are ideal for pouring liquids into the lip pocket, as is a clean, unbreakable syringe without the needle. Stroking the underside of the chin and throat area after the medication has been given will encourage your dog to swallow all of the liquid.

Pills and capsules: Giving your dog a capsule or pill can sometimes be a challenge to your resourcefulness. You can try to fool it into taking the medication by placing the pill inside some raw hamburger made into a small meatball, or in some other favorite food to disguise the taste. Some dogs will just eat them as part of their meal when put into their food. Most will not, unless they are real "chow hounds" and anything in their supper dish is devoured as a normal course of events. The most common method used is simply to open the dog's mouth by placing one hand under the jaw and one hand across

Heartworm and Lyme disease should be discussed with your veterinarian. Monthly medication is available to prevent heartworm, but be sure the treatment has been approved for collies as serious reactions to certain types of drugs have been reported. Inoculations are also available for Lyme disease prevention.

the top of the muzzle, applying a little pressure against the upper teeth and prying the mouth open. Keeping the capsule or pill in the hand with the lower jaw, simply drop it as far back on the top of the dog's tongue toward its throat as possible. Close its mouth immediately and begin stroking the throat to help it swallow. Be sure to watch it for a few moments afterwards to be sure it does not spit out the pill. If it does, repeat the procedure until the pill is gone. Occasionally, we have had a collie that would try to hide the pill away in his mouth until he was sure we had gone, only to come back and find the pill on the floor when we were sure he had swallowed it! If at all possible, avoid breaking up pills, because some pills have a protective coating that is important for delayed release in the intestine.

Managing Your Aging Collie

As your collie enters into its senior years, it will become less active, preferring to spend more time sleeping. Seemingly content to watch from the sidelines, it will observe activities without getting involved. It may have difficulty getting up and down the steps or from its sleeping quarters. Its legs will seem stiff as arthritis begins to affect the joints. Its appetite may or may not decrease but it will need a balanced diet of fewer calories and fat, a diet sufficient in protein, bulk, and essential minerals and vitamins. Consult with your veterinarian about the various foods manufactured for the senior dog.

There are several things you can do to make life easier for your senior citizen.
• Be sure that its bed is away from drafts. Give it some extra bedding to soften the impact of its joints against the hard floor surface. A foam rubber pad, covered with a washable material, will give the dog relief and comfort.

• Put its food and water bowl up on a platform several inches from the floor to make eating and drinking easier. You will want to fix this so the dishes can't fall off.
• Put down a piece of carpet for the dog to stand on while eating or drinking to keep the rear legs from slipping.
• Keep the teeth clean to help prevent painful gum infection that often occurs easily in older dogs.

The senior dog needs to be let out more often to urinate, unable to "hold it" for as long as a younger dog. Put down newspapers at night near the sleeping area in case it can't get outside in time. And don't scold it for using the papers or perhaps missing them; it will feel embarrassed enough. Keep the dog clean and well-groomed; it is essential for the older dog, to keep it free of objectionable odors. Frequently, the skin of older animals becomes dry and even scaly due to reduced activity of the oil-producing glands. If your collie is showing evidence of skin problems, consult your veterinarian.

Dogs never outgrow their need for the prevention of infectious diseases. The annual checkup and booster vaccinations are still an important part of their well-being. Your older collie should have moderate exercise. Excessive amounts should be avoided, and good judgment in evaluating the dog's physical condition and tolerance for daily walks and play is necessary. Also remember that extremes in weather are often hard for an aging dog to cope with.

When the End Comes

It is very hard to say good-bye to an old friend, one we have loved and who has loved us in return. Any pet that has become a member of the family has known a good life and will be missed. When your collie can no longer function in a way consistent

When the good days are over and the quality of life of your collie is less than satisfactory, it is your moral duty to ensure a humane ending.

with a quality life, or when it is in pain, you owe it the dignity in death you afforded it in its life. Your veterinarian can help you with your decision when the time comes. Today, euthanasia is a quick and painless procedure for your aging dog. Many veterinarians will let you stay with your dog until the end, even holding it in your arms if you wish. Don't be afraid to grieve for the loss of your collie. It is a tribute to its life and the fact that it made its presence felt in yours. Tell any friends who can't understand your grief for "just a dog," "He wasn't just a dog—he was my collie."

The Versatile Collie

Whether you want a purebred dog for a companion or for competition, the collie is a versatile breed equally suited for its many roles in service to humans. Collies have won recognition in all phases of conformation, herding, obedience, and agility competition. Collies also are famed as trackers, search and rescue dogs, therapy and guide dogs, and in drug detection. Collies have served with distinction in wars, and their valor is legendary.

The Collie at Work

The collie at work is a statement of the breed's capability beyond the show ring and obedience trial: "Collies are naturally protective. Any farm dog should be. What good are shepherds who let a thief steal their herd, or lets a predator kill or harass them? Collies can be taught to do serious protection very easily. The only problem with collies is they do not appear very threatening to people—I have never had one that showed its teeth at any person. They bark and stand between me and danger, but they do not snarl and snap, so collies do not appear menacing and many people try to 'call their bluff.' They are taught to guard my car, the house, the fence line and, when on leash with me, to 'alert' to any suspicious person, or violence. Yet, they 'turn off' instantly and will not 'alert' on children or people arguing in the home. They have a common sense to them that I have not seen in the protection breeds."—Kathy Stokey, "The Collie—Versatility with a Capital V." Courtesy *Collie Cues,* June/July l984.

The Herding Collie

Few activities offer the variety of situations and the opportunity for real teamwork with the collie than herding. The collie's origin as a herding dog, though not much utilized in that capacity today, survives with its herding instinct, despite engineered changes in the breed. It is a natural and precious attribute of the breed—the other side of the collie companion dog.

When the collie works livestock as herder and protector of the flock, its gentleness and compassion, strength and gaiety, and intelligent ability to read your moods serve it well with its sheep. Even the breed's gaiety is an integral part of its work, readily seen when the collie, with its rump in the air, tail wagging and barking, teases sheep out of a tight corner. The collie annoys one out and all the sheep immediately follow the leader.

Not all dogs born of working parents work and not all herding dogs want to herd. They must want to function as herders. A dog can be taught to do whatever you wish it to do. There are two distinct types of herding dogs. One is very strong and brash while the other is a soft dog who must be coaxed to a self-confident level of performance. A happy dog is one with a sense of responsibility and confidence. Even a shy, retiring dog, unable to cope with life outside its backyard, can be taught to herd sheep and walk away with a never-before-displayed cockiness. The dog is simply taken back to its origin and responds to a level of confidence that it had never known before.

The herding instinct test that follows seeks to discover the dog's natural ability. When a dog is used with livestock, it will clearly display one of the two herding styles, that of a "fetcher" or "heeler." Put another way, the dog will be either a gatherer or a driver. The test tells the trainer how the dog wants to work. Separating the chaser from the herder is related to what the chaser does with the item that it is chasing.

Livestock, preferably sheep or ducks, are used for the collie herding instinct test because the collie is an upright working dog and must learn to avoid the kicking hooves of cattle. When testing a dog for herding instinct, a dog must be given every chance to have a good first association with livestock.

What to look for in a working dog: What does the trainer/tester look for in the dog? It's the dog's response to the livestock. Is there immediate interest? Is the dog afraid to leave its owner? Will the dog be happier in a smaller area or a larger one?

Careful analysis of the dog's reaction to the livestock causes the trainer to introduce the dog to only one lamb, sheep, or duck, or perhaps three or five sheep in the pen. A dog may become intimidated by the whole process and head for the gate if it is in a very large area. Three sheep may scatter in many directions if a very strong dog dives into their midst. Adding one or two more to the flock may make them stand together. The dog must be assured by the owner as well as the trainer that it won't be scolded, that it is all right to go to the flock. Not all dogs respond to the livestock the first time out. Some will need further association. The goal is for the dog to realize just what it is that you expected it to do.

The collie is a "fetcher." On the other hand, it will heel when the handler is on horseback. After it has put the sheep or ducks in a tidy group by circling, the collie "fetcher" will turn the livestock back to the trainer.

After the collie has been tested and starts to work with sheep, it is time for the handler to practice some control. The idea is to displace wild, disorganized, random activity with constructive work for the dog. The handler is in command. Managed control is encouraged by actions and voice levels. This relates to the collie just how pleased the handler is by the dog's endeavors. A positive response to the dog usually makes the training process easier.

Herding training: Herding training is best done with enthusiasm. The result is a happy herding dog that is interested and challenged in its work. Later, content and at rest, the dog knows that it has done its work well. Every collie should have its day, in and apart from herding, to enjoy working with its master.

The training should always be geared to the dog's ability to handle the job assigned to it. A puppy or dog is never introduced to livestock that it cannot outrun. If it has not learned to "Sit" or the command "Down," the puppy must not be given a directional task. First things first. A puppy must learn to know livestock, then it is taught to "Lie Down" and the command "That will do" away from the livestock (the latter command, by the way, means "stop whatever it is you are doing and come to me"). Only then should it be started on livestock to see if it is ready to start to run. An adult dog should be handled the same way. It must learn its basic stopping and a call of command, "Down," so that it can work under some control. A handler must be able to read the dog. Too much control too early can turn the dog off.

Apart from the collie's gentle temperament, there is a variety of styles present as with any breed. Even when

A collie is gentle, loving, and has a protective nature.

The herding instinct of the collie is strong, and it will often manifest itself with unexpected subjects.

Few activities offer the variety of situations and opportunity for real teamwork than herding with your collie.

excited, collies are not inclined to bite. They rarely become overly anxious and aggressive, although some collies will be quite active and intense. Others are not quite as boisterous, yet still enjoy their work, while some collies can be downright lazy. The most desirable dog is eager yet sensible. A more excitable dog may cause a needless ruckus. Even the lazy dog is helpful in some situations, as with docile stock in a small area.

While broad, general training techniques and principles apply, most dogs are individuals and different methods will work best for different dogs. Many trainers do not begin more intense training with stock until a young dog is at least a year of age. The maturity of mind and body is inseparable and important. The dog learns from the handler and the handler learns from the dog.

Clinics: Herding instinct and training clinics are now offered in areas throughout the country. Participate with or without your dog. Help and learn. The trainer is there to get you off on the right foot. Trials can be fun if you do not take them too seriously and as long as you take them in your dog's stride. An important point to remember is that it is not your ego trip; you and your collie working together are a team. Enjoying this relationship as an accomplished herder or in the training stages is a rewarding goal for you both.

The qualities that make a good herding dog also contribute much toward making the dog an outstanding companion. A fascinating and gratifying activity, herding testing and training help preserve the collie's unique heritage as a herding breed.

Tests and Trials

The purpose of the herding test and the competitive herding trial program are defined by the American Kennel Club:

"—The purpose of the noncompetitive herding tests is to offer herding and breed owners a standardized gauge to measure their dogs' herding instinct and trainability upon exposure to livestock. The noncompetitive program begins with a basic introduction to livestock for dog and handler and progresses through gradual steps to requiring a dog to demonstrate that it is capable of being trained to be a herding dog.

"—The purpose of the competitive herding trial program is to preserve and develop the herding skills inherent in the herding breeds and to demonstrate that they can perform the useful functions for which they were originally bred. Although herding trials are artificial simulations of pastoral or farm situations, they are standardized tests to measure and develop the characteristics of the herding breeds.

"—Herding tests and trials are sports and all participants should be guided by the principles of good sportsmanship both in and outside the test and trial fields."

Competitive Events

In most sections of the country, there is some type of performance or conformation competition nearly every weekend. Events like obedience trials and tracking tests are measures of the collie's performance, while dog shows are evaluations of the dog's conformation.

Obedience trials test a dog's ability to perform a prescribed set of exercises on which it is scored. There are three levels of obedience classes, each more difficult than the preceding one:

1. The first level is called "Novice." To be acceptable companions, a set of Novice exercises comprise what all dogs should be trained to do. Among the exercises are heeling on lead, staying on command, and coming when called. A "leg" toward an obedience degree is earned when a competitor gets more than 50 of the points on each exercise and a total score of 170 or more out of a possible 200. To win the degree, three legs must be earned under three different judges. The Novice level title is called "Companion Dog" or "C.D." and is indicated after the dog's registered name.

2. The next level of obedience performance is open work, with such exercises as retrieving a dumbbell, jumping a hurdle, and the broad jump. The scoring is the same as for Novice, and the degree that is earned is the "Companion Dog Excellent" or "C.D.X." title.

3. Utility work is the most advanced level. Among the exercises that must be completed are scent discrimination and responding to hand signals, leading to the title of "Utility Dog" or "U.D."

Dog show judging is subjective. Remember this and be ready to try again.

The positive results of obedience training are dogs with good manners that last a lifetime.

A dog with the Utility title can continue to compete and, if successful, can become an "Obedience Trial Champion" or "OT Ch."

4. Dogs passing Tracking Tests, in which a dog must follow a trail by scent, earn a "T.D." or "Tracking Dog" title. "T.D.X." or "Tracking Dog Excellent" is awarded to dogs passing a more advanced test.

Obedience training and obedience trials are both worthwhile experiences. A dog with good manners is a good canine citizen and a welcomed member of society. The trial competition is a test of your ability as a trainer and the intelligence of your collie. Unlike conformation competition, your dog is not judged against other dogs; only its own ability is judged.

Dog Shows

Dog shows or conformation competitions are events given where each dog is judged according to a set standard or an ideal physical appearance approved for its breed. Judges compare the dogs and evaluate them according to the mental image of the "perfect" dog. There are two types of shows in which a dog can earn Championship points toward the title of Champion. One is called an All-Breed Show, where many different breeds of dogs are exhibited; the other is known as a Specialty Show for only one specific breed. Both types of exhibition are good places to see your favorite breed of dog. Find out more about showing collies beginning on page 58.

To get the names of local dog clubs that put on shows, obedience trials, or other performance events in your area, contact the American Kennel Club.

The Courageous Collie

Collies are conspicuous among the most courageous dogs in America honored as the Dog Hero of the Year. Beginning in 1954, the dog performing the most outstanding act of courage leading to the saving of life or property has been selected by a panel of highly respected judges. The annual dog hero search is sponsored by the Ken-L Ration division of the Quaker Oats Company.

The inaugural Dog Hero cited for bravery in 1954 was Tang, a collie who was honored for saving the lives of children by leaping in front of automobiles to push the youngsters out of their paths. Tang's magnificent courage has been equaled or exceeded through the years by countless dogs nationwide. These valiant dogs have saved more than 50 lives that we know of. They have fought off wild animals, prevented drownings, and alerted owners to fires and burglaries.

Among the many collie heroes was a white-faced dog named Blaze who, in 1957, saved a two-year-old girl from an enraged mother sow. The child had gotten into the pigpen and the sow had knocked her to the ground, severely mauling and biting her. Blaze leaped to the challenge and savagely charged the sow so that the badly injured child could crawl through a fence to safety.

In 1961, another collie hero, Duke, saved a ten-year-old girl whose skirt had flamed up in a backyard trash fire. The collie seized her blazing skirt in his teeth, tore and pawed the garment off her, and barked until the child's father rushed to aid his daughter.

In 1964, Buddie proved himself a true friend of humans and other animals when he herded his master's goats out of a burning barn.

A collie named Hero lived up to his name in 1966 when he saved his two-year-old master from being trampled by a wild horse.

Buddy, a mixed collie, was cited in 1989 for alerting a disabled grandmother to a house fire and thereby ensuring the escape to safety of the woman who had limited vision.

Collies care. The record of these valiant collies represents the breed's exceptional and often psychic feats.

A family of rough collies. Sire at left, sable dam and tri-color offspring.

War Dogs

The training of dogs for military and police work began in continental Europe toward the end of the nineteenth century. The abilities of the breeds of Great Britain attracted special attention. Collies were obtained from the Scottish Highlands for service as ambulance dogs in Germany. The German army also trained collies to carry messages. The Italians concentrated on collies for ambulance work, and collies were successfully used as ambulance dogs by the Imperial Russian Army in the 1904 war with Japan.

Britain: There was little interest in Britain in training dogs for police and military duties until the outbreak of World War I. Among other breeds, collies were considered desirable for guardian and sentry work because of their essential qualities of keen sense, high intelligence, courage, endurance, and trainability. Informally and unofficially, collies assisted police in their rounds; the Bobbies used their own dogs.

With the outbreak of war on the Continent, military authorities trained dogs for their armed services and provided dogs for their allies. Before going to the battlefields, the dogs were given extensive training for their duties—messenger, sentinel, ambulance worker—and exposed to smoke and gunfire.

Turkey: A memorable account relating to civilian adaptation and employment of dogs for protection duties is recorded in the exotic instance of collies deployed to Turkey. With their trainers they traveled there on the Orient Express to demonstrate their guardian prowess at the request of the Sultan. So well did the collies detect intruders, it was ordained by the Sultan that they remain in Turkey to help patrol the palace grounds and guard the Sultan's harem.

France: Dogs were sent to France to serve as messengers. The record indicated that of all the breeds used, collies were the most numerous. All

A smooth collie working as liaison dog.

utes to finish. The dogs worked in all conditions, from the extremes of weather to the roar and carnage of battle, over rough terrain and across obstacles such as canals, streams, and barbed wire.

Sentries: Collies also were excellent sentry dogs that accompanied patrolling soldiers, guarding supplies, and acting as area guards. Keen hearing and scenting ability were essential for sentry dogs. So as not to give away their position, the dogs were taught to give their warning in a low growl when on patrol. The dogs were not trained as attack dogs; rather, their protective abilities might become important and necessary in circumstances of defense—defense of the area, the dog's master, or for self-defense.

Helping soldiers: The savage carnage and intolerable conditions of trench warfare precluded widespread use of ambulance dogs on the battlefields. However, when called upon, the dogs saved many lives, ranging over the battleground, seeking out the wounded, and notifying their handler of the find. Sometimes the dogs worked on long leashes. They found and stayed with a wounded soldier and barked until assistance came, or they would return to their handler with an article belonging to the wounded man. Sometimes the dogs returned to their handlers, encouraging them to follow.

The advent of World War II brought a renewed interest and need for military dogs. Collies, border collies, English shepherds, and related breeds served as sentry and search and rescue dogs. Ultimately, contemporary technological advances effectively ended the job of the army messenger dog.

American forces: There were rough collies in the American armed forces during World War II, but not many as the rough collie's long coat and the care it required precluded their extensive use. Smooth collies, on the other

dogs were used with great success, including working and "show" collies, highland sheepdogs, and bearded collies. Collies were most often used as messenger dogs because they embodied the qualities required for such things—intelligence, endurance, high initiative quotient, and a strong sense of duty. Though speed was essential, reliability was prized even more highly. Carrying messages between other men and their handlers was the messenger dogs' primary duty. Liaison dogs also carried messages back and forth between handlers, with the written messages placed in a container on the dog's collar.

The dogs worked equally well at night and day, often completing their runs four times faster than human runners. A typical trip might cover two or three miles and required 15 to 20 min-

hand, were prized during both world wars because their short, hard coats required less grooming in the environments in which they served.

A part-collie, part-husky was one of the first army dogs sent overseas during World War II. Named Chips, he was the only war dog to receive an official United States military medal, the Silver Star, for his gallant service. He was on duty as a sentry dog during the 1943 Roosevelt-Churchill Casablanca Conference.

Dogs have continued to serve in every war through Desert Storm in the Persian Gulf. Though records are incomplete, some estimates suggest that upwards of 40,000 dogs have served with American armed forces, including about 20,000 in World War II. Dogs also saw service during the Korean War, and it is believed that the lives of some 10,000 U.S. servicemen were saved by dogs during the Vietnam War.

Although the army's Canine Corps was officially disbanded at the end of the Vietnam era, dogs are still used for sentry and patrol duties by some uniformed units, such as the Air Force, and as searchers in government facilities and for customs inspections.

Drugs: Other tasks, such as sniffing out drugs and explosives, are performed by dogs. The Honolulu, Hawaii police had great esteem for a trained collie, Candy, who did some astonishing work for the customs inspectors. Her owner, a member of the department, was observed by a police official practicing scent discrimination exercises with her. They experimented and learned that the collie could pick out marijuana from other odorous packets containing spices, tea, and coffee. At the customs office, Candy never made a mistake. Surrounded by hundreds of packages, the female collie pinpointed caches, helping the customs agents to track down suppliers.

Candy was a collie who specialized in saving people from themselves.

Rescue dogs: Among the rescue dogs of Switzerland, a smooth collie was notable and distinguished, and received a gold medal for his work in areas of this mountainous country. Qualified dogs are registered after extensive training to search for lost or injured people. Training for this work is quite rigorous and demands intelligent and physically well-conditioned dogs. Beyond obedience discipline, the dogs' training includes guarding, swimming, and jumping over obstacles. Dogs engaged in rescue work receive special taxing incentives for their owners; however, they may be called upon at any time by the authorities if they are required for work.

Highly trained search and rescue dog organizations are active in various parts of the United States and have been used extensively to locate lost children and earthquake survivors and victims. Dog rescue organizations can be located in your area by contacting local or state police offices.

The Assistance Collie

Collies have been used by humans for numerous tasks to help handicapped, disabled, or physically impaired people. Sometimes this is an organized activity. Often, it is an individual, spontaneous development between the owner and the collie. The breed's powers of perception, recognition, and responsible reactions, combined with its great loyalty, recommend the collie for this work. Both varieties of collies, because of their temperament, trainability, and adaptability, have been employed in service to the hearing- and vision-impaired. Although not often used today in formal guide dog programs for the visually impaired, earlier in the century, the collie was an admired breed for this purpose in Europe and America. Its

The collie's power of perception in combination with its great loyalty recommend the breed for assistance and therapy work.

Pet-Facilitated Therapy: Instances and reports of collies assisting people in Pet Facilitated Therapy (PFT) capacities are commonplace. PFT is the use of animals to help people with special needs. The collie's gentle, caring nature is particularly well suited to its role as a helpmate.

Dog-related therapy assistance extends to the needs of the elderly, alcoholics, abused, autistic, and latchkey children, the terminally and mentally ill, physically disabled, and others with emotional and physical problems.

The collie's easy transition from performing before and working with school children to joyously greeting nursing home residents is readily apparent. Collies have no problem moving from obedience and herding demonstrations to spontaneously welcoming new situations. Nothing surpasses the love and companionship a collie gives to a lonely person, sparking an interest-in-life response and a recognition that someone, a dog, cares in a nonjudgmental way.

There are many benefits of such pet-facilitated therapy. The unique bonding and sharing of dogs help brighten depressing days, reduce stressful moments, and fill the void of separations. The understanding and unconditional love that a dog provides give the lonely and depressed, a sense of being wanted, of belonging. Therapy dogs can be regular visitors or live-in residents of a home or institution. While almost any breed is acceptable, the collie's herding ability and traditional traits of calm, loyal, gentle protectiveness that endear the breed to all, make it an excellent therapy dog.

The "Lassie" image favors collies in therapy work. Children and elderly people, sometimes fearful of being hurt by a large dog, are more receptive to interacting with collies. When a

height and easy coat care, in the case of the smooth collie, is an asset for its work as an assistance dog.

An example of dogs' keen sense of hearing became readily apparent in our blue merle collie, Vince. No matter where he was on the property, he knew when the telephone was ringing. He became very excited, whining and barking until the ringing stopped. He has been known to nose the phone receiver off the hook when no one was at home. We often wondered how the caller reacted to our collie answering the telephone!

The Therapeutic Collie

Nowhere is the collie's compassionate nature better expressed than in the breed's service to humans as therapists. The ease in which collies slip in and out of numerous duties and roles is remarkable.

collie licks their faces and lies down beside them, children relax. Their elders remember and reminisce about collies they knew as children or read about in the Terhune books.

PFT dogs must offer a stable, sound temperament, and friendly disposition. They must be sociable, confident, and well-mannered, as well as trainable and adaptable to new people, situations, surroundings, and often vexing incidents. Most collies have a natural ability to take all of this in stride. A calm, mannerly, and obedient collie dispels apprehension and proudly exhibits its title as a treasured therapy dog ambassador.

Obedience training of dogs is not mandatory for the dog to become a therapy dog. Many fanciers recommend this, however, because of the assured, confident, and concentrated conduct that results when a dog knows what is expected of it and when it knows it can perform.

Your commitment: Apart from the collie's qualifications and abilities, a personal individual commitment is absolutely necessary before you undertake the exciting and gratifying challenge of training a therapy dog. Will you donate your dog, your time, energy, and emotion, and follow-through to this work? People will depend upon you— and your collie will depend on you. Ready? Here are some steps you can take to proceed down the path to successful pet therapy work:

1. You can get started with a group or as an individual. Your local humane society usually will know of area needs and may have such a program in place. They also may refer you to local participants who can give you an idea of what is involved.

2. Find a support group with similar interests. Two major groups are: Therapy Dogs International and American Working Collie Association (see page 90 for address).

3. There are different pet therapy need areas that may or may not be suited to you and your collie. Can your collie handle the noisy, active child in a school environment? The sedentary nursing home frequently presents a range of emotions. Contact several facilities, explain your idea, and schedule visits without your dog to get a better feeling for you and your collie's involvement.

4. Having chosen your Pet-Facilitated Therapy area, and a support group, you and your collie need to be recognized and accepted into an area facility. Personally arrange an appointment and request a tour of the facility. Describe the program you want to provide and why and what you hope to accomplish. Keep an open mind and consciously strive for two way communication. Listen for the facility needs and ideas about how you and your collie can fulfill these needs. Complete any necessary paper work and ask to meet pertinent staff with whom you will work. Try and visualize how your dog will see the facility. Be aware of the environment, the structure, equipment, and apparatus— whirlpool bathrooms, wheelchairs, or oxygen tanks, if visiting a nursing home. Even a well-mannered, well-trained dog may be "spooked" by guttural noises and pained faces.

5. When you and your dog are ready to become familiar with objects such as canes, crutches, and carts that you observed on your facility tour, you should practice with a borrowed wheelchair or walker, at home or in some other relaxed atmosphere. Imitate or duplicate erratic sudden movements and noises. Your collie cannot possibly ignore every new, unanticipated situation, but, at the very least, it will not disdain new surroundings and people.

6. Introduce your dog to the facility with a short visit. Have the facility director accompany you and your dog

The love, patience, and continuous companionship collies give to their masters often become critical therapeutic factors.

Has it visited and greeted a number of new faces? Has it given its all to those who need it? Remember that your collie will do its best if it is fresh and energetic. Never do strenuous or stressful activity before or after therapy.

Pet-facilitated therapy is a formal way of contemporizing the human-dog relationship, interaction, and experience. There is no more rewarding and stimulating high for an owner and his or her collie than sharing their special bond together, enriching the lives of others.

The Carting Collie

The use of dogs in harness, pulling a small child or two, or a light load of firewood, reappeared on the American scene during the 1970s. Carting enthusiasts, while small in number, conduct the sport in humane and orderly fashion. Collie carters report that the breed adapts quickly and responds eagerly to the opportunity.

Contemporary carting with dogs is really an extension of obedience training and performance. There also is the added invaluable physical conditioning the dogs receive. A period of regular physical exercise with ever-increasing demands improves both muscle tone and strength. A well-conditioned dog should pull over a substantial distance on reasonably level terrain at least one and a half times its weight. Team carting with two or more dogs is a way to induce feelings of responsibility within the dogs.

Minimal equipment is necessary for carting. Apart from a well-maintained dog, a properly fitted cart and harness are essential. Ideally, the cart should be perfectly balanced with zero tongue weight, and should be flexible and inexpensive, a vehicle that all large and medium-sized dogs can pull.

A word of caution if you want your collie to take part in carting: This is an event for adult dogs only. Starting a

to meet the staff and residents. By acquainting your dog with the environment before working in it, you will build the collie's confidence and reaction to various situations and sounds. Support your dog by positively encouraging it. There is never a substitute for praise— "Good girl," or "Good boy."

7. Have a well-defined goal before each visit. Calmed preparedness will help you and your dog relax. Keep visits brief, not more than an hour, preferably once a week.

8. Always keep an eye on your dog when visiting. Respect your dog's needs, especially if it shows signs of nervousness, fearfulness, or stress-panting. If it does, take a break outdoors or in a quiet place. You may have to cut short your visit. Its attitude or conduct and your response or support really determines whether you have accomplished your goal and had a successful visit.

Do not overwork your dog. Has it been touched or petted constantly?

puppy in harness before full maturity could have serious consequences in its development. Talking to someone involved in carting before you begin training will help you get started correctly and avoid accidents or injuries.

Winter Sports

Skijouring and dog-sledding are sheer fun and sure-fire winter activities for both owners and collies.

In skijouring, the collie pulls the skier on cross-country skis. The key to an easy pull is to gradually introduce body weight to the dog's harness, before the skier actually assumes an upright position on skis. Apart from appropriate clothes, the equipment consists of skis, poles, dog harness, gangline belt or hand-held towrope. The sport can be adapted for non-snow conditions, with skis on rollers used for summer downhill practice.

Collie sledding enthusiasts say their dogs love the sport. They praise sledding with their dogs and relay the impression that their dogs enjoy working with and pleasing their partners. Team size can range from one dog to several. Most starters use from one to three dogs. The major equipment used is the dog harness and sled. A three-wheeled vehicle or rig is used when there is little or no snow. A team of well-conditioned adult dogs can easily pull an average-sized person. Collie sledding fanciers say it becomes increasingly difficult to hold back the dogs once they are exposed to sledding as the dogs are eager to go and they thoroughly anticipate the experience.

Skijouring and sledding with collies is a fun and efficient way of muscling up young collies and toning up maturing ones. At the same time, the fresh air and outdoor exercise stimulate and charge up both handler and dog.

Contact the Collie Club of America or the American Working Collie Association for more information on these sports (see page 90 for addresses).

The Collie as a Show Dog

The majority of collies are, without doubt, sold and owned as family pets; however, many are outstanding examples of the breed and are exhibited in competitions held around the country.

Both rough and smooth varieties of collies are exhibited as show dogs in competitions held around the country.

In general, people become involved with the showing and breeding aspect of the dog world after they have owned a particular breed and find they are interested in the competitive nature of the sport. Attending dog shows, both all-breed and specialty shows, is a good way to learn what they are all about. Some shows are held inside; some are given outdoors. The events are advertised in newspapers, usually the classified section, area pet supply stores, grooming shops, veterinarians' offices, and boarding kennels. Local breeders will also know about shows in your location. Magazines published about dogs such as *Dog World,* found in bookstores and stores selling general interest magazines, and *Pure Bred Dogs/American Kennel Gazette,* available from the American Kennel Club by subscription, publish names and dates of all AKC shows and obedience trials.

Dog shows are good places to talk to breeders and exhibitors about collies. Time your conversations and questions well before the scheduled hour collies go into the show ring or after the classes are finished as a great deal of attention must be given to the dogs before judging, and concentration by the handlers is understandably intense. Spend some time watching the grooming and preparation, staying well back from the area so as not to get in the way. Because a great deal of consideration is given to the way a dog looks while it is being judged, it is considered bad manners to touch or pet a dog being groomed.

Most exhibitors will be happy to talk with you and answer questions when the atmosphere is more relaxed.

Purchasing a collie with showing and breeding potential is not much different from buying a companion dog for your family. Care and early training are a major part of any dog's life, show dog or otherwise. A reputable breeder offering show stock can be found by contacting the American Kennel Club or the Collie Club of America. The club's secretary will put you in touch with a director for your state who will be able to assist you in locating a breeder.

Understanding the reason for dog shows, and the breeding of purebred dogs is necessary before you can fully appreciate the concept relating to this sport. As stated earlier, selective breeding for the collie as a specific breed began many years ago. When the breed was sufficiently recognized for its particular characteristics, a breed standard was written. This is the accepted blueprint for what a collie should be, not only in physical terms, but in temperament as well. The standard was written keeping in mind the collie's work as a herding dog and the necessity of soundness in movement (i.e., its ability to move correctly without tiring). The head and expression of the collie are of particular importance in demonstrating type, the characteristic that makes it different or sets it apart from any other breed.

The basic information we provide on the collie standard on pages 62–65 will help you realize how much thought and knowledge go into responsible breeding. Maintaining the integrity of the breed is of utmost importance.

Collie puppies that breeders feel are the most likely candidates for showing are kept by the breeder for further perpetuation of the family traits, or sold to a show home. If you are

Proud tricolor smooth collie at a show.

interested in obtaining a show prospect puppy, your breeder can become your best and most valuable resource. The price for a show dog is significantly more than you will pay for a companion dog and the seller will want some assurances that you will indeed exhibit the collie sold to you.

On the other hand, not every puppy showing potential will turn out as expected. Relying on the breeder's best judgment is about all you can do until you become knowledgeable enough to

Noise and close proximity may get anybody nervous. This is a common situation that requires calm and careful handling.

The social rules of the wolves affect the modern dog and its behavior. By establishing yourself as the pack leader and by using good eye contact, you will increase your collie's attention span and ability to learn.

choose for yourself. Sometimes, trial and error seems to be the answer. In order to better ensure your success in the show ring, an adult collie that has already been trained for show and, in fact, may already have achieved some points toward its championship, is a better investment. Such dogs are expensive but save you time and, in most cases, money in the long run.

Showing off a beautiful dog is fun. But your entire family should be in agreement about the commitment needed to take part. Competition in dog showing is no different than competition in any other sport; it is a combination of learning, luck, skill, and will. By far, the greatest thrill of achievement is to create through your own knowledge a breeding program and family of dogs that consistently meets the challenge of competition in the show ring.

Learning to train your collie for the show ring can be done in training classes offered by local all-breed clubs. These classes are usually open to the public, charging only a minimal fee for each lesson. All-breed and specialty clubs (clubs dedicated to a specific breed) give matches as well as regular AKC licensed shows.

A match does not offer points toward a championship but rather acts as further training opportunities for puppies, older dogs, handlers, judges, and club officials. The dogs are divided into classes by age and by sex. A fun match will allow puppies as young as two months of age to participate, but the puppy should be inoculated before taking part in these events. This informal show is a fine opportunity for you and your puppy to learn about dog shows and to meet people in your chosen breed. Exhibiting at matches will help you get ready for the big leagues.

Understanding Dog Shows

Attending a dog show for the first time can be an overwhelming experience. If it is an all-breed show, there will be great numbers and varieties of dogs to see. While bewildering at first, you will soon get the hang of things and more than likely want to return again and again to cheer your favorite dogs to victory.

The primary purpose of a dog show is to enable owners to exhibit their dogs in competition with others of their kind, and by using only those dogs that have proved, through such competition, to be the best representatives of their breed, to improve the quality of purebred dogs.

Dog shows that are licensed by the American Kennel Club are subject to strict rules that must be adhered to by everyone connected with the show. All dogs must be purebred, six months of age, and registered with the American Kennel Club to enter a licensed purebred dog show. They are considered adults on the day they become one year old. Puppy classes are usually divided by age as well as sex. The first classes are for the six to nine month olds and nine to twelve months.

There are seven groups into which dogs are placed, according to the work they do and type of dogs they are: Sporting Group, Hound Group, Working Group, Terrier Group, Toy Group, Non-Sporting Group and Herding Group. There is a Miscellaneous Group that consists of breeds not presently recognized by the American Kennel Club. These dogs may compete in that class only and may not compete in group judging or earn championship points.

Judging Order: The collie is in the Herding Group. Before the Best of Breed collie winner can compete against other dogs in the Herding Group competition, it, like all breeds of dogs, must be judged against its own kind in classes divided by sex. Male dogs are always judged first. When these classes have been judged, the female, or bitch, classes begin and are judged in the same manner. The winners of these classes meet again and are judged best male and best female. These two winners now compete against dogs that are already champions. From these dogs are chosen the Best of Breed, Best Opposite Sex to the Best of Breed, and Best of Winners.

Winning points. Only the two winners from the classes, male and female, can win the points for the day. These points accumulate each time they win at any AKC licensed show. The maximum number of points to be won in a single show is five. The number of points is determined by how many dogs are entered in the show—the more dogs, the more points. In order to become a champion, the dog must accumulate 15 points under three different judges.

To finish a championship, the dog must win a minimum of three points at two different shows. Three points or more are called majors. In other words, a minimum combination of six major points and nine minor points are required.

There are no points awarded in the group judging. But a win or placement in group competition carries a great deal of prestige. The Best of Breed or Best of Variety winner of each individual breed is eligible to be judged in its own group. Only the winners of each of the seven groups meet to determine the Best in Show, the ultimate achievement for the day.

Single-breed shows: Single-breed shows, or specialty shows, are judged in much the same way, except that there is no group judging. At a collie specialty show, as in an all-breed show, the rough and smooth varieties are judged separately. The Best of Breed winner rough and the Best of Breed winner smooth both appear in the Herding Group judging. At a specialty show, the Best of Variety

smooth and the Best of Variety rough compete against one another for Best of Breed. Another exception is that the puppy classes and open classes are divided by color as well as by age and sex. There is also a class for puppies twelve to eighteen months of age. Otherwise, the judging procedure is done in the same manner.

Entering: To enter your collie in a licensed show and compete for championship points, you must first obtain an entry form. These forms are available from show superintendents or from club secretaries. A list of these sources are available from the American Kennel Club. The entry form must be filled out and an entry fee mailed by a specified date to the superintendent or show secretary. A week or so before the show date, you will receive a confirmation of your entry, an assigned armband number that you will wear while showing your dog, and a ring number if it is an all-breed show. Upon arrival at the show, there will be a table at your assigned ring where you can pick up your armband. Be sure to take your confirmation with you. If there are any mistakes on the form, you can tell the show superintendent at that time. Double-check the time of your judging—judges will not generally wait for latecomers. It is up to you to be on time with your collie, ready to present it in its class. So that you will know how to keep track of what is going on, you should purchase an official show catalog. It contains all the pertinent information about the dogs, their owners, handlers, classes, and the number of points to be awarded. There are also spaces provided to record the numbers of the dogs that are winners.

Grooming for shows: At most shows there will be an area set aside for grooming. In this area you can set up your grooming table, your dog crate, and the items you will need for

In junior showmanship competition, the handler rather than the dog is judged.

How Dogs Are Judged

The judge must study each dog carefully, with the hands as well as the eyes, with the dog in motion as well as standing still. He or she checks on the texture of the coat, firmness of muscle, and overall body structure, and also checks the teeth and the way they fit in the mouth. The head and expression of each dog must be evaluated and, in some cases, correct temperament as well. The judge is guided by the breed's standard and looks for the dog that, in his or her opinion, most nearly fills the criteria set by this standard. Placements are awarded from one through four to those dogs that best meet these requirements. The judge must also watch for definite faults that are to be discouraged or penalized in the breed.

Junior shows: In some shows, there may be classes offered for Junior Showmanship. This is open to youngsters between the ages of ten and seventeen. In this category, the handler, rather than the dog, is judged, so no championship points are given. However, a first place win entitles the boy or girl to move on to more advanced classes. Junior Showmanship is a recognized event by the American Kennel Club and often is the training ground for many of today's best dog handlers.

The Collie Standard

Official standards for each breed eligible for purebred dog registration are prepared by the parent or national breed club and approved and published by the American Kennel Club. A breed standard is a word description of what the ideal dog of that breed should look like. It is an attempt to describe "perfection." In their efforts to breed better dogs, breeders use these standards as their guides. Judges use the standards as guides when evaluating dogs at shows. The official collie

the day. Of all the things you will need for your collie at the show, none is more important than a container of water and a water bowl. Dog shows are stressful for the dogs and the owners, and every effort should be made to create as calm an atmosphere as possible. You are responsible for keeping your grooming area clean. Be sure to pick up any loose hair and place all debris in trash containers provided. If the show is held indoors, and grassy exercise areas are not available, fenced runs with plastic drop cloths covered with sawdust or cedar shavings are available on which your dog can relieve itself. These areas are frequented by a great number of dogs and it is impossible to know if any of them might be ill. People are warned not to bring sick dogs to the show grounds as a courtesy to other dogs, as well as safety for their own. Now is the time you really need to have those important inoculations working. If your collie must use these public comfort stations, stay with it and clean up immediately afterward. When you get back to your grooming area, wipe its feet off with an antiseptic. If you have taught your collie to "potty" on command, your trips to the "bathroom" will be very short.

standard was adopted by the Collie Club of America and approved by the American Kennel Club on May 10, 1977. You may obtain it by requesting the *Official Standard for the Collie* pamphlet to the American Kennel Club (see address on page 90).

The aforementioned guide indicates that the rough collie is a strong and responsive dog, who stands naturally straight and firm. As defined by the AKC, "The deep, moderately wide chest shows strength, the sloping shoulders and well-bent hocks indicate speed and grace, and the face shows high intelligence."

Male collies are from 24 to 26 inches (61–66 cm) at the shoulder and weigh from 60 to 75 pounds (27–34 kg). Bitches are from 22 to 24 inches (56–61 cm) at the shoulder, weighing from 50 to 65 pounds (23–30 kg). Penalties for undersize

or oversize collies depend on the extent to which they appear to be undersize or oversize.

The head should be light, never massive. Both in the front and profile view, the head resembles a well-blunted lean wedge, with a smooth outline. On the sides it tapers gradually and smoothly from the ears to the end of the black nose, without flaring around the brain case or pinching in the muzzle.

The teeth should meet in a scissors bite. Overshot or undershot jaws are undesirable, and the latter is more severely penalized.

The eyebrows have a very slight prominence. The backskull is flat, without receding either laterally or backward, and the occipital bone is not highly peaked. The correct width varies with the individual dog and depends on how much is supported by the length of muzzle.

Because of the importance of the head characteristics, prominent head faults are severely penalized.

A blue merle rough variety female with very distinct markings.

A consistent winning show record recognizes an outstanding representative of the breed. This beautiful tricolor male is a good example.

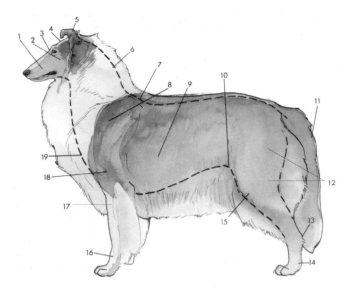

The neck is firm, muscular, and frilled. It is considerably long and carried upright with a slight arch at the nape.

Expression is one of the most important characteristics of collies, yet it is very difficult to define. It is the combined result obtained after judging the shape and balance of the skull and muzzle, the placement, size, shape, and color of the eyes, and the position, size, and carriage of the ears.

The body is firm, with well-sloped shoulders and deep chest that extends to the elbows. The back is strong and level, supported by powerful hips and thighs.

The forelegs are straight and muscular. Both narrow and wide placement are penalized. The hindlegs are less fleshy, muscular at the thighs and very sinewy, and the hocks and stifles are well bent. The feet are comparatively small. The soles are well padded and tough, and the toes are well arched and close together.

The gait is sound. When the dog moves at a slow trot toward the observer, its straight front legs track comparatively close together at the ground, without a choppy or rolling gait. The same applies to the hindlegs when viewed from the rear. As the speed of the gait is increased, the collie single tracks, bringing the front legs inward in a straight line from the shoulder toward the center line of the body and the hindlegs inward in a straight line from the hip toward the center line of the body.

The tailbone reaches to the hock joint or below. The tail has an upward twist and is carried low when the dog is quiet. When gaited, or when the dog is excited, it is carried gaily, but not over, the back.

The coat is abundant everywhere except on the head and legs. The outer coat is straight and harsh to the touch. A soft, open outer coat or a curly outer coat, regardless of quantity,

Anatomy of the collie.

1. Muzzle
2. Cheek
3. Stop
4. Skull
5. Ear
6. Neckline
7. Withers
8. Shoulder
9. Rib cage
10. Loin
11. Tail
12. Ear
13. Hock
14. Rear pastern
15. Stifle
16. Front pastern
17. Forequarters
18. Brisket
19. Chest

Except in the case of blue merles, the eyes are required to match in color. Eyes are almond-shaped, of medium size, and should never appear to be large or prominent. Their color must be dark. The haw, or inner eyelid, sometimes is white or light-colored rather than the preferred dark color, but it should never be so prominent as to affect the dog's expression.

In blue merles, dark brown eyes are preferred but either or both eyes may be merle or china in color without specific penalty. An eye that is large and round works against the expected "sweet" expression of this dog. Consequently, eye faults are heavily penalized.

The ears are in proportion to the size of the head. When in repose, the ears are folded lengthwise and thrown back into the mane. When the collie is alert, they are drawn up and held three-quarters erect.

A dog with stiffly upstanding ears or with low ears is incapable of showing true expression and is penalized accordingly.

is penalized. The undercoat, however, is soft, furry, and so close together that it is difficult to see the skin when the hair is parted. The hair on the tail is very profuse; on the hips it is long and bushy. The texture, quantity, and fitting of the coat are important points.

The four recognized colors are sable and white, tricolor, blue merle, and white. There is no preference among them. The sable and white is predominantly sable (a fawn sable color of varying shades from light gold to dark mahogany) with white markings usually on the chest, neck, legs, feet, and tip of the tail. The tricolor is predominantly black, carrying white markings as in a sable and white; it has tan shadings on and about the head and legs. The blue merle is mottled or marbled color, predominantly blue-gray and black with white markings as in the sable and white; it usually has tan shadings as in the tri-color.

The rough collie's distinctive mane accounts for easy identification of this variety.

The white is predominantly white, preferably with sable, tricolor, or blue merle markings.

The smooth collie is judged by the same standard as the rough variety, except that the references to the quantity and distribution of the coat are not applicable to the smooth variety, which has a short, hard, dense, flat coat of good texture, with an abundance of undercoat.

Whether the collie is smooth or rough plays no significant role in dog shows. However, in the past several years the smooth collie, although somewhat less well known than the rough variety, has been gaining in popularity as a family pet because of its shorter coat and ease in grooming.

A beautiful rough white collie with blue merle head.

Breeding Your Collie

The concept that a female dog must be bred and have a litter of puppies to be psychologically fulfilled is not correct. In fact, a neutered female collie makes an outstanding companion. She is able to give all her time and attention to her human family. If you have purchased a female collie with the thought of breeding her, just to have puppies or to get back some of the purchase price, you are on the wrong track.

The art of breeding dogs is not an easy one. Consideration must be given to the conformation and temperament of the dogs. Allowing two collies to mate, even though they are both purebred and have registration papers, will not necessarily ensure a litter of quality puppies. A good knowledge of the breed and the breed standard (see page 62), as well as some understanding of genetics, should be a prerequisite to any breeding program.

Before you decide to breed your female collie, you and your family should consider carefully the time and expense of raising a litter of healthy and active puppies. Stud fees are set by the owner of the male dog and vary in price, depending on the popularity of the dog as a stud, his pedigree, and the consistent good quality of the puppies. Veterinarian fees should be figured into the budget. The female will need an examination before breeding and should be up to date with all her inoculations. Fecal exams will be necessary to be sure she is free from internal parasites. She will need a prenatal exam and additional food and supplements to produce enough milk for the whelps. Puppies will need to be checked and probably wormed, and at least the initial shots given. Eyes will need to be checked and registration papers obtained. Special puppy food diets and supplements must be purchased when the litter is three weeks of age. As little appetites grow, increased amounts of food will be needed to meet their demands.

Another factor to think about is where these puppies will be sold and the homes they will go to. With today's problem of overpopulation in dogs, the market for purebred dogs in your local area may not be very strong. This will mean advertising them in out-of-town newspapers or breed magazines in order to find the right kinds of homes for them.

The importance of finding good homes for your new puppies cannot be stated often enough. Another good reason for working with an established breeder is that they will often put people in touch with you after your female has been bred and you can begin a waiting list of potential clients. This will give you time to talk with the interested buyers and find out just what they are looking for and what they expect from you. This is also a good time to find out about the environment your puppy will live in, whether or not they have a fenced yard, and who will be responsible for the new puppy. Price should not be discussed at this time, but parties should be called after the litter is born and everything looks good. An appointment can be made several weeks after the birth of the puppies to introduce yourselves and them. It is wise not to take deposits on unborn puppies; promises made at this time cannot always be fulfilled and unnecessary problems will surely arise.

To successfully breed purebred dogs, it is important to begin with a mental grasp of what it is you are trying to accomplish. The preservation of as many good qualities of the breed as possible is essential to your success. All of these good qualities must be preserved in the next generation of the breed to insure the integrity of the collie as an individual type of dog. To deviate from this principle would create an undesirable type of collie and eventually the very special qualities so important to the breed would diminish.

As a novice breeder you would do well to contact the owner of the litter from which you purchased your female collie puppy. At the time you bought your puppy, you may have discussed the possibility of breeding her. Assuming that this person is a reputable breeder, you should be able to talk with him or her and get information and suggestions about breeding your collie. Often, this breeder will ask you to bring the female back to the kennel to be bred to a collie relative or one that he or she feels would be a suitable mate for yours.

In any event, you will certainly want to talk to as many collie breeders as possible and visit as many kennels as you can, to see what is being produced by the sires you may plan to use. Doing your "homework" ahead of time is important. Sometimes, reservations are required for the more popular studs. Be sure to ask about this. Using the most popular stud dog is not always the right way to go. This particular dog may not "fit" with yours in terms of a genetic background or, in some cases, will double up on a specific fault. You will need plenty of help and advice, and of course, your veterinarian is a good source, too.

Types of Breeding

There are three types of breedings to consider when you decide to enter the world of dog breeders. The first is called inbreeding. This refers to a litter having the same dog on each side of the pedigree or matings of parent to offspring, or brother to sister. When you breed two dogs with a common ancestor, their litter inherits some of the same genes from each side of the pedigree. This allows for the probability that genes will "double up."

Most breeders prefer to avoid inbreeding. This close relationship may cause some undesirable traits to appear that, once set strongly in the line, are hard to be rid of. A knowledge of the faults and virtues of all the common dogs in the pedigrees for at least three generations is required when considering inbreeding.

The second method, linebreeding, is the safest and best way to preserve conformation and the most favorable qualities of the breed, providing that the dogs chosen to mate have the essential characteristics necessary, and that the breeder is capable of selecting the best puppies from the litter for future breedings. Linebreeding is accomplished by breeding two relatives in the same bloodline, but not as close as described in the inbreeding combination. Most commonly found in linebreeding are matings of grandparents to grandchildren, cousins or nieces and nephews to aunts or to uncles.

Using two dogs from entirely different bloodlines for breeding purposes is called outcrossing. Many breeders will use this method after linebreeding for several generations. Outcrossing is used to introduce new genes into a bloodline for a specific purpose. The outcome of the litter is less predictable and the uniformity is not as great, but many times the results are surprisingly good.

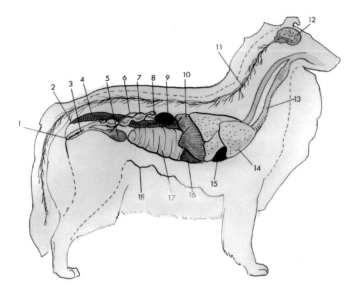

Internal organs of the female collie.
1. Vulva
2. Anus
3. Vagina
4. Rectum
5. Bladder
6. Ureter
7. Developing embryo
8. Ovaries
9. Kidney
10. Liver
11. Spinal cord
12. Brain
13. Trachea
14. Lungs
15. Heart
16. Stomach
17. Intestines
18. Teat

The Female

A female used for breeding should be in top physical condition. One that is overweight and not accustomed to exercise is difficult to mate. Often, she will not come into season on a regular basis and may have difficulty whelping a litter.

Generally speaking, it is not wise to breed your bitch before two years of age. Waiting for the second or third season will ensure that she has reached emotional maturity and is able to adjust well to the role of a good mother.

Most female dogs come into what is commonly called "season" between the ages of six months and one year. During that time, the bitch is preparing herself for mating. She will come into this cycle every six months or so, beginning with her first season. You should be able to track her seasons fairly accurately. For instance, if your bitch has two seasons seven months apart, she will probably follow this pattern throughout her breeding life. A severe illness

or surgery will sometimes alter this pattern, but she will undoubtedly go back to her original schedule.

Estrus: The most common cause of unsuccessful mating is breeding at the wrong time during the estrous cycle; therefore, you should have a good understanding of how the cycle takes place.

The heat cycle or estrus lasts for 21 days. It is calculated from the first sign of vaginal bleeding and is divided into three parts. The onset of heat is called proestrus and lasts from six to nine days. During this time you will notice a firm swelling of the vulva, accompanied by a dark bloody discharge. At this stage the female begins to attract male dogs who are able to detect the odor from a chemical substance discharged from the vulva in her urine. She will not accept a male during this time. Should you attempt to breed her during this time, she will jump away, sit down, growl, and snap at the male to chase him away. Sometimes fights will occur if you allow the male to stay with her.

The next stage of the estrous cycle is known as estrus or standing heat. This stage will last from six to twelve days. During this time, the female is receptive to the male. She will begin to flirt and twist her tail to one side. When touched in the rear, she will flag her tail and lift her pelvis to present her vulva. The discharge changes from bright or dark red to a pinkish color, and sometimes will appear almost clear or the color of straw. At the same time, you will be able to see that the vulva has softened while remaining quite swollen in size. At this time, it is wise to take her to the veterinarian for an examination of the discharge to determine when she will be ready to breed.

The third phase in this cycle is metestrus. It begins when the female will no longer stand for the male and

A dog used at stud must be in top physical condition.

will end her breeding cycle. She should be kept away from other dogs for the full 21 days unless, of course, she is to be bred.

It is quite normal and natural for some females to develop a false pregnancy (pseudocyesis) 60 days after estrus, if she is not bred. She will show all of the classic signs of being in whelp—increased appetite, weight gain, swollen teats, and enlarged abdomen. She may even drip milk, nest, and fill the nest with toys she can cuddle. Often, the false pregnancy stops if you take the toys away and she has nothing to cuddle. Reduced food intake and increased exercise will help get her back to normal in a short time.

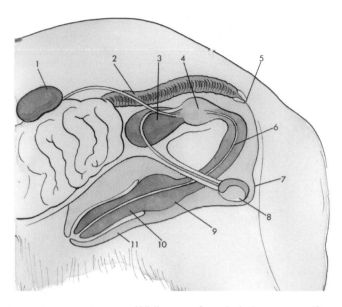

Internal organs of
the male collie.
1. Kidney
2. Rectum
3. Bladder
4. Prostate
5. Anus
6. Urethra
7. Scrotum
8. Testicle
9. Bulb
10. Penis
11. Sheath

While your female is in season, if she is not to be bred, as during her first season or two, you must make plans to keep her indoors and away from neighborhood dogs. Once the scent of a female in season is noticed by the male dog population, you will find a number of previously unknown dogs in your yard. Unless your neighbors cooperate with you and keep their dogs at home, it can create a terrible nuisance for everyone. The dogs will sit outside your door for hours at a time, day and night, howling and sometimes pawing and scratching at your door to get inside. On warm days, when your doors and windows are open, it is not unheard of to have strange dogs attempting to jump through the screens to get to your female.

After the twenty-first day, and before she is allowed to be with other dogs, she should be given a bath. If not bathed, the heavy scent of estrus remains with her and males may still believe she is sexually active. Nature encourages males to mate on scent alone.

The Stud Dog

Male dogs, not unlike females, will lead a perfectly happy and healthy life if they are never bred. In fact, they will probably make better companions if neutered at a young age. They certainly will be more willing to stay at home and mind their own business rather than checking out all the neighborhood females.

Many pet owners call breeders and kennels offering their dog at stud. The response is always a negative one because breeders have their own breeding programs and they usually have their own studs. Advertising him at stud in national magazines, and in most cases local newspapers, is a waste of money. There are a great many top quality stud dogs available so, unless your collie happens to be one of those with outstanding qualities, he will not be used.

A consistently winning show record is generally the first criteria for a male to be widely used at stud. His recognition as an outstanding example of the breed by many judges and his ability to produce winning offspring set him apart from all the rest. Indiscriminate breeding of either males or females should be avoided under any circumstances.

Physical Condition: A dog used at stud must be kept in top physical condition at all times. High protein diets with vitamin and mineral supplements added to his daily food ration are necessary to keep him at his best. The dog should not be too fat; in fact, a lean dog will breed more easily than one that is overweight and sluggish.

Inoculations: The stud dog's inoculations must be kept up to date and routine examinations for internal and external parasites done. The veterinarian should do a periodic fertility test or sperm check. The sperm count should be high and the sperm very active. Any illness or other influences such as injury, worm infestation, or intense summer heat can reduce fertility.

If you are breeding your female, watch her carefully when she is due in season. As soon as she shows a bloody discharge, you must contact the owner of the stud dog. All arrangements should have been made well in advance for the mating. Be sure the terms of the breeding are understood before you send your female to the stud dog owner. Most stud fees are paid at the time of the breeding. If your female does not conceive after the breeding, some stud owners will offer a return service free of charge. This is not mandatory and will depend on the kennel you choose. Sometimes, if your collie is of outstanding quality, the owner of the stud dog may ask for a "pick" puppy as payment for the stud fee. Any terms are best put in writing to avoid later misunderstandings.

When you contact the stud owner, he or she will tell you when to bring your female to the stud dog. It may be desirable to have her there right away so that she can get settled in before the mating. Most stud owners are experienced in knowing the right time to breed and are less likely to miss her ovulation if she is there in plenty of time. If you are breeding your collie with a local or nearby stud, it will probably be convenient for you to drive her to him and leave her for a few hours or overnight. This will mean several trips for you because females are usually bred two or three times, a day or so apart. If she is to be bred a long distance from home, it is best to drive her to the stud early enough for the stud owner to keep her until she is ready to breed. Be sure she is well brushed out and free of ticks and fleas. Nothing is worse for stud dog owners than to receive a female into their kennel with these unwanted pests. You should take pride in presenting your healthy and beautiful collie to another collie owner.

Kennels: In the world of stud dogs, it is "lady's choice." Since females are brought to the males for breeding, the stud dog owner must have appropriate kennels for visiting females, inside kennels that are escape-proof and away from your other dogs. Visiting females must also have an enclosed exercise area where they can be taken under close supervision.

Records: If you are the owner of the stud dog, you must keep accurate records regarding the breedings and anything of an unusual nature that might occur. Be specific about the dates and time of matings and whether or not the female was easy to breed. Use a calendar to record appointments made for your stud dog so that he is not used more than once or twice a month. Overuse of a stud dog will almost certainly render him sterile. Telephone the female's owner after the mating has been accomplished to set a time for her to be picked up. It is best to keep a bred female for a day or two if she has a long distance to travel. This will allow her time to rest before the trip.

Breeding area: Your stud dog should have a specific area for breeding purposes. He should be taken there only when a female is ready to be bred. If he is allowed to visit this place at such times, and at no other, he will be psychologically prepared each time he is taken there. The area should be a pen or fenced-off portion inside your basement or garage, away from other dogs and distracting noises and activity. An outdoor breeding place is not recommended. It often takes quite some time before the breeding occurs and would be very uncomfortable in case of rain, extreme heat, cold, or snow.

Feeding: Do not feed either the female or the male before the breeding is to take place as it could be upsetting to their stomachs. In any event, you want them to be alert and excited, not feeling full and satisfied, ready for a nap.

Mating

To accomplish a successful breeding two things must occur. The female must be ready to accept the male, and the two dogs must be compatible. There have been many disappointments when, for whatever reason, the two dogs involved simply did not like each other. Under these circumstances, they may be introduced to different partners, and a mating will occur quickly and without incident.

When the mating pair meet, there will be several minutes of playful negotiations or flirting, half-hearted attempts by the stud dog to mount the female, as if testing her willingness, and a lot of twisting and turning around one another.

The dogs should never be left alone. If possible, it is advisable for two people to attend the mating, one person to hold the female and keep her still as the stud dog mounts, and another to hold her tail to one side. Occasionally, a maiden will have to be muzzled for the first several minutes of penetration by the male. Do not be alarmed if she should cry out at first or make sounds during the breeding. This is natural. Males do not generally like to have someone assisting. They should be trained from the first time to have the owner present, helping the dogs as needed.

Once the male has penetrated the female past the sphincter muscle ring in the vagina, the bulb at the base of the penis is temporarily locked in place. The two are joined together and cannot separate. At this time, the male ejaculates sperm that is deposited in the cervix. A few minutes after the two are tied, he will turn his rear leg over the female's back and they will stand rear to rear until they separate naturally. Both the male and female may

The collie falls into the medium-size range. Having most of the attributes of a big dog, it is not one, and only appears so because of its big coat. A very amenable dog with its own kind, the collie thrives on human companionship and seems to reason better than most other dog breeds.

have to be supported during the tie. Do this by placing your arms under their rib cage to keep them from attempting to sit down. They will move around to keep their balance. It is important that they are not standing on a slippery surface. A long piece of heavy carpet or a ribbed rubber runner will offer good footing for them. The tie can last from a few minutes to an hour but the normal amount of time is about 20 minutes. Do not attempt to separate the dogs before they have completed the breeding as serious injury to both of them can result.

After the breeding is finished, allow the male to lie down for a few minutes. Take him back to his kennel or living quarters, give him a drink of fresh water, and let him rest quietly by himself. An hour or so later, feed him a substantial, high-protein meal. He should not be kennelled near the female or her scent may cause him to refuse food.

The female must be removed from the breeding area at once. She should be kennelled or crated to keep her from urinating for at least an hour or so. Offer her a drink of water and let her rest by herself, away from activity and any distraction that could cause her to become excited or stressed. Her regular ration of food should be given at her usual feeding time.

The owner of the female will send the stud dog owner a litter registration form to sign after the litter of puppies has been born. The owner of the sire of these puppies, must sign the papers and return them immediately. If the stud dog owner is to take a stud fee puppy, he or she should make a selection by eight weeks of age so that the litter owner is free to offer the rest of the puppies for sale. A contract drawn up ahead of time, with all the specifications of the agreement, will forestall any problems at this time.

Pregnancy and Whelping

Gestation: The period from conception to birth is called gestation. It averages 63 days. Puppies born on the fifty-ninth or sixty-sixth day fall into this range. Puppies whelped before the fifty-seventh day will be too small and probably will not survive.

Signs of pregnancy: It is difficult to know if your female is indeed pregnant. Large breeds, like the collie, carry their puppies well up under their rib cage. Collie females tend to grow more coat after they are bred, making it even more difficult to see positive signs of puppies. At about five weeks into the gestation period, there is a noticeable change in the nipples as they begin to enlarge, and the breasts appear fuller. The belly hair begins to shed and the area feels warm to the touch. We like to see the vulva stay a bit swollen or puffy and a slight clear or even milky color discharge continue after the mating. This has proved to be a good sign that the breeding has been successful. Other signs of pregnancy are increased appetite and enlarging abdominal girth. Some people say they see a definite change in personality. An unmistakable indication of puppies can be found at about six or seven weeks. When your female is lying on her side at rest, place the palm of your hand flat against her side just above her breasts. Keep your hand there without applying pressure for several minutes. The warmth of your hand will cause the whelp to move. At first, it feels like a slight ripple under the skin. As the whelp grows stronger each day, the movement will be more pronounced. It is possible to get a fairly accurate count of the expected whelps a few days before they are actually born.

Good condition: Keeping your expectant collie in good condition is very important. Her eyes should be bright and alert, her coat shiny, and

Heated box for newborn puppies. Make sure temperature is right ahead of time!

her gums a healthy pink color. She should not be allowed to become too fat and she should have routine daily exercise. Pregnant females should not roughhouse with other dogs or take part in strenuous play activities with members of the household. A brisk walk two or three times a day will keep her muscles toned and in good shape for the birthing process.

Feeding: During the first half of her pregnancy, feed your collie her usual ration of food. Increase the amount by one half during the second half of her pregnancy, as her protein requirements will increase. Always feed her a high quality food to be sure she is getting the proper nutrition that is absolutely necessary to produce healthy puppies. Talk to your veterinarian about the need for supplements or extra vitamins.

A week or two before delivery, your collie may show a decrease in appetite. It is better to feed her two or three smaller meals at this time than one large one.

Drugs: During pregnancy, certain drugs must not be given. They include

73

flea and insecticide sprays and powders, dewormers, certain hormones, and antibiotics. Be sure to tell your veterinarian she has been bred in case the need for medication should arise.

Grooming: Keep her clean and well brushed, but bathing her at this time is not recommended. Lifting her in and out of a bathtub could result in injury to an unborn whelp or to the mother.

Drafts: She should be kept out of drafts, kept cool in summer, and comfortable in winter. She will probably appear to be warm and pant more than usual as the weeks go by. This is normal for a female in whelp. Very often, the female will find a special place in the house, a sort of hideaway, where she can sleep, away from the hustle and bustle of the everyday family life. Toward the end of the gestation period, she will spend more time sleeping, resting and gathering the strength she will need to give birth to her puppies.

Getting Ready

While you are waiting for the birth of the puppies, assemble the articles needed for whelping a litter. A whelping box is the best place in which to deliver puppies. Construction of the box can be done at home or you can purchase a box from a pet supply store. The box should be at least 4 by 4 feet (1.2 × 1.2 m) in size, large enough for the dam to lay down comfortably but not so large as to let all of her body heat escape. They are usually made from plywood and consist of four sides fitted together and screwed into a floorboard. If you fasten the sides together with hooks and eyes, the whole box can be taken apart and stored flat. Three of the sides should be about three feet high and the fourth about one foot high. This will make it easy for the dam to get in and out of the box without having to jump in, perhaps landing on a sleeping puppy. This side can be replaced with a high-

er one when the puppies are older. We usually paint our boxes with a high gloss enamel (be sure the paint is lead-free), which makes the box very easy to keep clean, washing it with a mild soap and rinsing with water. Towel-dry the box and everything is fresh again. A ledge around the inside of the box, a few inches from the floor, has saved many a puppy from being rolled on by its mother. The ledge can be made by nailing 3- to 6-inch-wide boards on all four sides. Puppies seem to crawl under these rails instinctively and are protected from being unintentionally smothered. To find the correct rail height, have your collie lie down in the box and measure against her side to see how high the rail should be.

Several layers of clean newspaper can be laid on the bottom of the box to absorb moisture and odor. You will use a lot of newspapers in the coming weeks so start saving them now. Store the papers in plastic bags to keep them clean. We don't use the color pages because of the dye.

Decide where the puppies are to be born. The area should be quiet, warm, and draft free. An unused room would be good so that the door can be closed and the mother can take care of her new family undisturbed. Warmth is one of the most important factors in keeping new puppies alive. The floor temperature should be 85°F (29°C) for the first seven to ten days of life. Keep a thermometer handy to check the temperature frequently. When the pups are a week or so old, the temperature can be decreased by five degrees weekly until 70°F (21°C) is reached. By then they should be up on their feet and moving around and their internal body temperature has stabilized. To keep the temperature at 85°F (29°C), you may need to use a 250 watt infrared heat bulb, either securely suspended above the floor of the box or mounted in a floodlight reflector. You will have to gauge the height of the bulb with your thermometer resting on the floor of the box to check the temperature. Be sure to leave space out of the direct source of heat for the mother to rest in a cooler area if she wants to. All electric cords should be out of the box and situated so that no one can trip over them. If the room becomes too dry with the extra heat, hang a wet bath towel in the room to add some humidity.

Introduce your collie to her new sleeping quarters a couple of weeks ahead of time. Coax her into the box and tell her to stay in it for a few minutes. She probably will not want to stay there for long so don't insist on it. This is not a place to go for punishment. Take her there every day, praising her for staying in the box for any length of time. In a few days, she will be willing to at least stay in the room with the box, if not in the box. As the time draws nearer, you will find her sleeping there and fully accustomed to the idea of her new area.

Another whelping article you will need is a smaller cardboard box with a towel-covered heating pad on the bottom. You can place the newborn puppies in this box while others are being born. Test the heating pad ahead of time for the right temperature. The towel should be warm but not hot enough to burn the puppy. The box can be placed alongside of the whelping box or inside the big box if the new mother becomes too anxious about her puppies being away from her.

Also have on hand:
- a rectal thermometer
- some sterilizing solution
- petroleum or lubricating jelly
- dental floss or white nylon thread
- a small pair of forceps
- blunt-tipped scissors
- antiseptic, such as iodine to apply to the umbilical stumps

- paper towels
- a supply of freshly laundered towels
- absorbent cotton balls
- plastic trash bags
- plenty of fresh newspapers

We also use a baby scale to weigh the puppies and keep a notebook handy to record the date and time of birth, sex, weight, color, and markings.

Whelping

A few days before the puppies are due, your collie may exhibit signs of restlessness, wanting to go in and out more often than usual, occasionally scratching at the floor or rearranging her newspapers. This is called nesting—a sure sign that whelping will begin in a matter of days. Her appetite may fall off and she may refuse any food. Leaving half-portions of food for her to eat whenever she is hungry is enough for now. On the other hand, some females will eat up to the last minute and never miss a meal. Plenty of fresh water is necessary and some

A change in behavior and marked interest in the whelping box are signs that puppies will soon arrive.

Female groomed before giving birth.

a day or so before she is due, may help you to know within a few hours when she will deliver. It is easy to miss this two degree temperature drop. A normal temperature does not mean that she will not whelp.

Over the years, we have had two females that did not want to whelp their puppies in the whelping box. We knew they were ready, but they continued to pace and acted as though they wanted to get in a closet or under something. Finally, we understood that they wanted a den or cave in which to have their babies. We put a table over the box and draped a blanket down to cover the sides. Both times, each mother went willingly into the "den" and settled down to deliver her pups. After the first puppy arrived, she was satisfied to stay in the box without the curtains. However, when all her pups were delivered and she had taken complete charge of her new family, we dropped the blanket down again, leaving one side open so that we could observe the situation from time to time. In a day or so, we took the table and blanket away and she was content in her "nest."

Labor and Delivery

As the labor process begins, your collie will become extremely restless, panting heavily, tearing and pushing the newspapers around in the whelping box. There will be a mucous discharge from her soft and swollen vulva. She may jump in and out of her box, circling around, looking anxiously at her hindquarters. Sometimes, a female will try to nip at herself as the puppies begin to move down the birth canal. Now is the time to put her in the box, getting her to lie down. This is sometimes hard to do, especially for a female having her first litter. Talk to her in a soothing voice and stay close at hand. Keep other people out of the room; loud noises and strangers in the

will like to drink a little milk from time to time. She will need to urinate more frequently now so be sure she can get outside to relieve herself as often as necessary.

This is a good time to cut away any long hair around the nipples and on her belly. Comb through the "skirts" on her hindquarters and cut a sort of heart-shaped opening in the hair around the vulva. We trim off some of the hair on the underside of the tail for sanitary reasons and to keep the puppies from becoming entangled in the long hair. Wash her whole abdomen with warm water. If a mild soap solution is necessary, be sure to rinse the area thoroughly and dry it well with a soft towel.

Most females whelp their litters between 60 and 63 days. It is important to find out from the stud dog owner on which days she was bred. You will need to plan the time from the first breeding through the last, sometimes a difference of several days.

Eight to twelve hours before the delivery, her temperature will drop from a normal of 101°F (38°C) to 99°F (37°C) or below. Taking her temperature with a rectal thermometer early in the morning and again in the evening,

area will delay the whelping. Most litters are whelped at night or in the early hours of the morning, nature's way of keeping distracting influences to a minimum.

Most dams have their puppies unaided, needing only light supervision to see that all is going well. When delivery is imminent, the female will become increasingly agitated. She will pant with her tongue out, lick her vulva, and strain as if trying to have a bowel movement. The first puppy is usually preceded by a burst of water-like fluid. Eventually, a transparent, fluid-filled umbilical sac is presented with a puppy inside. You must watch carefully to see that the mother tears open the sac immediately so the puppy will not drown. If she seems not to do this instinctively, you must quickly help her break open the sac by first tearing away the membrane around the head. Keep the whelp near her face so that she will hear the first cries of the newborn. Usually, this is enough to stimulate her into action and she will begin to lick the whelp and remove the rest of the sac herself. As you tear open the sac keep the head of the puppy down so that fluids can drain from the lungs. Gently open the mouth and wipe out any remaining fluids.

The dam should now take over and chew the cord away from the placenta. If she appears disinterested or too tired to help with the puppy, carefully tear away the rest of the sac. If the placenta is still attached, clamp the umbilical cord near its center with the forceps, then tie the cord with dental floss or white thread about an inch or two from the puppy's abdomen. Be careful not to stretch the cord from the puppy, causing an umbilical hernia. Tearing the cord rather than cutting it is recommended to prevent bleeding. Remove the clamp. Then use your fingers to milk the blood toward the placenta, severing it above the knotted thread.

Put iodine on the jagged edges of the remaining cord. The cord will shrink as it dries and will fall off in a few days. Rub the puppy briskly with a dry towel until it wiggles and cries. Give it back to the dam putting it up to her side to nurse. She should take over from now on. If not, follow the same steps with each puppy until she does.

As each puppy is born, take the previous pups away and place them on the towel-covered heating pad while the mother is taking care of the current pup. This will keep the puppies from becoming chilled and wet. Tiny puppies have no shivering mechanism. They cannot warm themselves and many puppies are lost due to chilling. Screaming is a signal that puppies are too hot, as opposed to a whimper when too cold and angry yells when they are hungry.

Each time you put the pups back with their dam, encourage them to nurse. She will lick them over and over again to stimulate them. You will be

The dam will chew the umbilical cord away from the placenta. Help her if she looks too tired or disinterested.

followed by an afterbirth—a retained placenta will cause a uterine infection in a very short time. When whelping is finished, your veterinarian will administer a hormone to stimulate contractions of the uterus, and thus "clean her out."

Newborn Puppy Care

After you feel relatively sure all the puppies have been delivered, the mother will need to go outside to relieve herself and move about. It is sometimes difficult to convince her to leave her puppies but it must be done. Use a collar and leash, if necessary. Place all the pups in the cardboard box on the heating pad while you are gone. The soiled and wet newspapers should have all been discarded and fresh layers of papers laid down. We try to put new papers down after each pup is whelped if time allows, keeping the box as clean and dry as possible. Don't be alarmed if the dam rearranges the papers when she returns to the whelping box. Put the puppies back in the box with the mother. She will "count" each one with her nose, and set about cleaning them again. She normally will have a slight discharge for several weeks, so keep her off the carpet. This is nothing to worry about and will gradually disappear. If you should see fresh red blood, it could mean a serious internal injury, in which case you should consult your veterinarian.

After whelping, the dam will probably be hungry and ready to eat. Some milk should be offered, and a full meal a bit later. A soft diet for a day or two, with some added canned meat to encourage her appetite, and she should soon be ready to eat her regular food. She will need about two or three times her normal food intake while nursing. Dividing it into feedings of three or four meals per day is preferable. Feeding ample food during the three or four weeks that she is

Once the pup is separated from the umbilical cord, rub it with a towel and give it to the mother.

amazed at how quickly they learn where the faucets are and how to make them work.

In a normal delivery, puppies are born at intervals of ten to thirty minutes or not more than an hour apart. If you think there are still unborn puppies, take the dam outside on a leash to relieve herself and to have a short walk around the yard. The exercise and a drink of water may help things along. Take a flashlight along if it is dark and do not leave her unattended. It is not unusual for a puppy to be born outside. If whelping does not seem to be progressing normally, call your veterinarian. Do not let your female struggle unproductively for more than an hour or so.

Opinion is divided on allowing the dam to eat the placenta (afterbirth). Generally, she should be allowed to eat at least the first one if she shows an interest in doing so. You may remove the placentas as each one is expelled but be sure to keep track of them. It is important that each pup is

providing all of the puppies' nourishment is essential to good milk production. Also, be sure she has a plentiful supply of fresh water available.

During the first 48 hours after the birth of the puppies, your job is to make sure each puppy is getting on a teat and sucking well. Most newborn puppies instinctively find the source of food and start nursing on their own, but you may have to help one or two by gently opening their mouth and placing them onto the nipple. Expressing a few drops of the dam's milk onto their tongue may help give them the idea. You might have to hold them on the teat for a few seconds until they get a firm grip. Very often, we find that a puppy will have a favorite "station." No matter how many times you try to put it on another nipple, it will return to its favorite place.

It is important for puppies to get the dam's "first milk." This rather watery-looking secretion is called colostrum. It is richer in protein and fat than her later milk and contains antibodies that protect the puppies against certain infectious diseases, such as distemper. This maternal antibody protection gradually wears off but by then the puppies are ready to start their own immunization program.

Enter the weight of each puppy in your notebook and update it every week for the next month or two. Weight gain is one of the best means of determining how well your puppies are doing. Most of them will lose an ounce or two in the beginning but should at least quadruple their birth weight during the next three or four weeks. If you are concerned that a puppy is not doing as well as it should in the first 24 hours, ask your veterinarian about supplementary feeding program. The simulated dam's milk formulas on the market are excellent and are easily purchased from either your veterinarian or a pet supply store.

Every time the mother returns to the box she will count the puppies with her nose.

Observe the details of the whelping box—especially the protective ledge built inside.

Check your puppies frequently to be sure they are all getting their fair share. In a big litter the smallest are likely to be pushed aside by their littermates. Let the smaller ones nurse a few times each day, with the others kept away. It won't take long for them to catch up.

Tiny puppies cannot automatically eliminate so you must be aware of the mother aiding in this function. She should roll them on their backs and lick their abdomens and rectal area to stimulate urination and defecation. All puppies are born with a wax-like plug in their rectum. This must be evacuated with the help of the mother. Occasionally a puppy will hang back and cry for no apparent reason. Use a cotton ball dipped in warm water and gently wipe the anus in an upward motion under the base of the tail for a few minutes until you see the plug being expelled. If it continues to cry and seems too weak to eat, seek professional help. The dam will keep the whelping box clean for her puppies by eating their feces and urine. She will do this until they are weaned to solid food.

As soon as the puppy can see, an irresistible curiosity sends it to discover the world. At this stage they are innocent and foolish; be ready to help and protect.

During the next three weeks there is little for you to do except to keep the mother supplied with nutritious food and fresh water, check the room and box temperature, and change the newspapers as needed. Putting a large bath towel or mattress pad cover in the box over the papers will give the puppies better traction when nursing. We put a heating pad, covered with a towel or receiving blanket tucked around it, in the whelping box. The puppies will gravitate to the warmth and pile up on it. As they become warm enough, they will separate and lie stretched out, comforted by the consistent heat. Wash the towels or pad covers as they become soiled.

Puppies should be left alone as much as possible to sleep and grow. Excessive handling is detrimental and may introduce infection or cause injury.

Visitors: When a visiting breeder expressed an interest in seeing our new litter, we ignored our rule of not showing newborns to outsiders. The visiting guest did not attempt to handle the puppies but we did spend a good deal of time discussing them. Before long, the mother left the box to stand with us. She was a friendly collie and I thought nothing of the fact that she seemed to want some attention and petting. We patted her head as she leaned against us, slowly circling around our legs. Much to our surprise, the new mother had gently but firmly moved us away from the box and was "showing us the door."

Behavior: Normal, healthy puppies sleep soundly between nursings and twitch and jerk in their sleep. They have no problems crawling toward or locating their mother and their sucking instincts are strong and vigorous during nursing. Normal puppies seldom cry. Their bodies are warm and when picked up they should feel firm and solid. They should squirm and resent being held in your hand away from the warmth of their mother and littermates.

Health: A puppy that is limp and feels cool or clammy to the touch is in trouble. The coat looks dull and feels harsh and they may have yellow diarrhea. Many times, the mother will reject such a puppy, sensing it is not right. Warmth is the first and most important consideration for this pup. Remove it from the whelping box and put it in a small box with a warm hot water bottle wrapped in a lightweight material. Put a towel three quarters over the top of the box to help retain the heat. Move the puppy from time to time and rub it gently with a terrycloth towel to help its circulation. It takes a while to get the body heat back up where it should be. When the puppy begins to move around in the box, try to give it a little honey, and boiled warm water, about a teaspoonful given slowly with an eyedropper on the tongue. Be sure it swallows before giving it more. If it responds to this, put it back with the dam and try to get it to nurse. It may be necessary to put the heating pad alongside the mother for the puppy to stay on for a while. If you cannot bring it around, a trip to the veterinarian is in order. Keep the puppy on the towel-covered hot water bottle in a covered box while you travel.

Developing: Puppies are born blind and deaf. At the beginning of the third week, the eyes and ears are open, and their baby teeth are beginning to break through the gums. As they begin to stagger around the box, it is especially important to have secure footing for them. A slippery surface inhibits their ability to get up on their feet properly and could result in injury to hips and shoulders. In just a few days, they will be toddling around, staging mock battles with their littermates.

Teeth and nails: The first canine teeth often are referred to as milk teeth. These little teeth are sharp, and so are the pups' toenails. The dam will put up with them surprisingly well,

but in consideration of your devoted collie mother, you should do her the favor of keeping those dagger-like toenails cut short. A pair of human nail clippers will do the job nicely. You will probably have to do this when the mother is out of the room as she will not like the fact that you are trying to help her out.

Food: Between the third and fourth week, you can introduce a soupy mixture of food—baby meat and cereal mixed with undiluted canned milk or bitch's substitute formula. We have

Socialization begins around the fourth week, when the puppies establish relationships with their littermates.

used the strained lamb baby meat with rice or oatmeal cereal as a starter. Dipping your finger in the soup, take one puppy at a time and rub some of the mixture around the inside of the mouth. Try to get each one to lick the food from your finger. Do this for a day or so and they will soon be ready to lap from a small dish or saucer. The best way to start the dish routine is to hold the dish up to the puppy while it is standing and allow it to get its face in the soup and lick the dish clean. This way it cannot get its feet into the dish. Working with each pup individually for a few times, until it gets the hang of it, will make the group feeding easier. We elevate the food an inch or so off the floor of the box until the pups are really good at eating on their own. Depending on the size of the litter, feeding three or four puppies from one pan encourages them to eat more quickly and to stay with it until all the food is gone. Watch to see that each pup is getting a fair share. Keep a damp towel handy to wipe off those sticky faces. The mother will help you out for a while but, as this mixture dries, it hardens and acts like glue. Keep a container of water available for the pups once you have started the weaning process. A Pyrex loaf pan filled about two-thirds full is heavy

Portable puppy playpens with interconnected panels come in various sizes.

enough so that they cannot tip it over and high enough to keep them from stepping in it. Press their noses just to the top of the water. They will snort and shake their heads but eventually they will learn to lap the water. Keep the water dish in the same place so they will grow accustomed to finding it easily.

Socializing: The fourth week of the puppies' development is a critical time as socialization begins. They start to establish relationships with their littermates as well as with humans. You will see them wag their tails at each other, bark, and start to play. When you come into the room and speak to them, they will begin to recognize your voice and acknowledge your presence. They should be handled and talked to frequently. Leave a radio on in the room for part of the day, alternating music and talk show programs. Soon they will respond to other people and new sounds. Moving their quarters to an area where they will get a lot of attention and handling will help them to socialize with human beings in the future. Putting an exercise pen attached to the whelping box, perhaps in the kitchen, will give them both a bedroom and a play area. You may select a portable, folding exercise pen from various models offered with connected panels, usually two feet in width, and in various heights. We generally use a 36- to 42-inch-high pen so it can be used for an adult dog as well. They can be opened up and fastened to each side of the cage with metal snap-lock fasteners. As they are already accustomed to sleeping in the box, they will start to use the outside area as a bathroom. Remove the front panel from the box so they can get in and out easily. Keep plenty of newspapers on the floor for quick cleanups. This is a first step toward housebreaking.

Weaning: Weaning should be well underway during the fourth week.

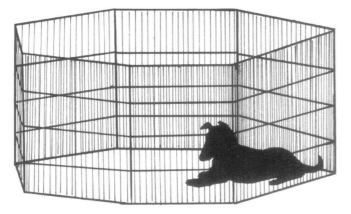

Gradually increase the amount of solid food at each feeding. The dam will be more willing to leave them for longer periods of time, but will still want to check on them periodically.

Begin weaning with one or two meals a day, letting the mother nurse them for the remainder of their feedings. Within a few days, they should be eating three solid food meals and then four until they no longer need their mother for nourishment. As the puppies nurse less, the dam's milk will diminish and she will dry up. Cutting her food ration back to the normal amount, or even less, for a few days will help her to dry up more quickly. By five weeks, the puppies should be eating on their own and she should be taken away from the puppies totally. The puppies will still need to be kept out of drafts but their body temperature will be in the normal range.

Adding food: Between five and six weeks of age, puppy food or kibble can be introduced. Commercial puppy food is advisable for the next several months, as it provides more essential elements for fast-growing pups. We usually begin to introduce puppy food by grinding it for a few seconds in a blender before putting it into their feed pans. We soak it in some undiluted canned milk for a few minutes and they seem to love it. Gradually add water to the milk until it is half and half. If you notice that the puppies have loose stools, reduce the water content and start again. At six weeks they should be able to eat the kibble without your grinding it up and without the milk, soaked only in water for a few minutes. Some puppies prefer it dry by this time.

However you feed them, start slowly in order to avoid intestinal upsets. Using a high-quality puppy food is expensive, but it is money well spent in the long run. A healthy, "blooming" puppy is much easier to care for than one that is doing poorly and needs additional supplements to bring it up to par.

Sometime within the four to six week period, you will need to take a fecal sample from the puppies to the veterinarian who will check for internal parasites. Roundworms are the type most commonly found in puppies. If this condition is present, the veterinarian will give you medication for the puppies. The pills usually work quickly and have no side effects. A second sample will be necessary as a follow-up measure to be sure there is no further sign of these parasites. Your veterinarian will then give you a schedule for the pups' first inoculations.

Do not try to worm or inoculate your puppies with over-the-counter vaccines or wormers. Your veterinarian is a professional, trained in methods of treatment necessary for your puppies. A miscalculation on your part could have devastating results.

Eyes: Any time after five weeks, you must make an appointment with a qualified canine ophthalmologist to have your puppies' eyes checked for collie eye anomaly (see below). You can find such a specialist listed in the yellow pages of your phone book, from your veterinarian, or from local breeders in your area. As a conscientious collie breeder, you are obligated to the breed to have the eyes of all your puppies examined and to forward this information to prospective buyers.

Eye diseases include:

1. Collie Eye Anomaly (CEA): Dogs as well as people are subject to inherited eye diseases. Two problems that affect the collie should be of concern to all ethical breeders. The anomaly, or abnormality, is present prior to birth, and unfortunately is found in a great number of collies. Much has been done over the years to lessen these numbers and ongoing research into modes of inheritance is being conducted at

Something that medical practitioners have already realized is the fact that our physical and emotional life is significantly enhanced by the bond formed between animals and ourselves.

major universities and veterinary schools across the country. Breeders can help to further eliminate the problem by breeding non-affected dogs.

When you take your puppies for their eye examination, drops are put into each eye to dilate the pupil. The interior of the eye is examined through an ophthalmoscope by a canine ophthalmologist. This procedure must be diagnosed by a trained observer.

Simply put, the anomalies affect the retina and include degeneration and retinal detachment. The degeneration is graded by the severity of the problem. Detachment results in blindness. Each eye may be affected differently; i.e., one eye may be only slightly affected, while the other has a retinal detachment. If there is degeneration, unless it is near the hemorrhage stage, it will not progress as the dog grows older. The majority of collies that are slightly to mildly affected have perfectly adequate eyesight throughout life.

Puppies are ready for their new homes at eight to ten weeks of age. They should be healthy and robust, and with an outgoing personality.

2. Progressive Retinal Atrophy (PRA): This disease occurs in many breeds of dogs. PRA is the term used to describe retinal degeneration that eventually results in total blindness in both eyes. It is important to be sure that there is no evidence of PRA in the dogs close to yours on the pedigree you received when you purchased your collie. Do not hesitate to ask the stud dog owner about the existence, if any, of PRA in the background of his dog.

Generalized PRA is not usually present at birth. As its name implies, it is a degenerative process. Early signs of the problem may be present as night blindness; the dog may have trouble seeing in dim light. While we have suggested your puppies be examined for collie eye anomaly as early as possible, they should be looked at again at six months for possible signs of PRA, especially if the dog is to be used for breeding or has any history of the disease in its family. An expert may detect early onset at six months or even younger.

Medical research into the mode of inheritance and gene identification is being studied by several veterinary schools and researchers in the field of canine ophthalmology. These studies are largely funded through donations to breed club foundations, such as the Collie Club of America Foundation, the American Kennel Club, the Morris Animal Foundation, and many others.

Separation: At eight weeks of age, puppies are ready to go to their new homes. They should be healthy, robust and outgoing in personality. This is an emotionally difficult time. Interviewing people to find the right homes for your puppies and parting with them is both a happy and sad experience. Remember how excited you were when you bought your first collie and how you looked forward to your relationship. Watching the expression on the face of a new collie puppy owner will tell you that all the sleepless nights, the dirty newspapers, and the routine of puppy raising, has been well worth the experience.

Orphan Puppies

Newborn puppies that have lost or been separated from their mother require a great deal of attention. If there is someone in the household to help you and split up the feeding schedule, it will make things much easier. If the separation from the dam is only temporary, she can later be of some help to you also.

Keeping puppies warm, clean, and fed will be your responsibility. A uniform environment must be maintained to prevent chilling. This can be accomplished through room temperature and an overhead infrared heat lamp or heating pad (see page 74 for temperature information).

The box you put the puppies in must be large enough to support the number of puppies in the litter, allowing enough room for the heating pad and space for them to crawl away from it when they become too warm. Wrap the heating pad in a towel. Be careful to secure all the folds and seal it tightly so that the puppies cannot crawl in between the cover and the heating pad. We like to place rolled-up bath towels on the floor around the edges of the box, much like bumper pads around a playpen. Safety pin the edges of the towel to the rolled portion so they cannot be opened up or crawled into. The puppies will need uninterrupted sleep and excess handling should be avoided. Except for feeding and cleaning, it is best not to disturb them.

If the mother is available but cannot feed them herself, she will probably be glad to help with the cleaning, at least for a while. If cleaning is left to you, rub the puppies occasionally with a damp washcloth. Dry them well. If the

heat from the lamp or heating pad causes dry skin, use some baby oil or lotion. As you are rubbing them with the washcloth, gently roll them back and forth from their tummy to their back as the mother would when she licks them.

Feeding: Orphan puppies need to be fed every three hours for the first several days. As you see them progress, and if the formula is agreeing with them, you can stretch out the time to four hours between feedings. By the age of ten days they will probably be able to get through the night for several hours without food. At two weeks, if the weight gain is consistent, you will be feeding them four or five times a day until three weeks, when their eyes are open and a gruel-like meal can be introduced. You will need a formula for the puppies that meets their nutritional requirements. A good supplement to use as a substitute for the dam's milk may be Borden's Esbilac or ICN's PuppyLac, in powder or liquid form, both providing a balanced blend of proteins, fat, carbohydrates, vitamins, and minerals. You can make your own emergency formula from materials on hand: a can of evaporated milk, one-quarter of a can of water, an egg yolk, a pinch of salt, and a few drops of human infant vitamins. The formula should be mixed well and stored in the refrigerator until needed, warming only as much as you will use in one feeding.

Bottle feeding is the best method of hand-rearing a puppy. It takes more time, but the benefits of sucking are more natural to the puppy and they seem to thrive. However, if the litter is large, bottle feeding at every feeding becomes a nonstop chore if you are doing it alone. You will need a regular baby bottle and premature baby nipples or orphan lamb nipples. Do not enlarge the hole too much, as puppies will not nurse if the milk comes too quickly.

They become just as discouraged and give up if the nipple is clogged. Hold the puppy on your lap with its front feet elevated on a small pillow or rolled towel. As it sucks on the nipple, it will begin to knead the pillow or towel, much as it would its mother's breast. When its sides and tummy look somewhat distended, you know it has had enough. Hold it on your shoulder to burp it, as you would a human baby.

After each feeding rub a cotton swab or cloth-wrapped finger, dipped in oil, over the genital and rectal area to induce urination and elimination. Do this for a week or, until the puppies are functioning on their own. If the dam is willing, give the puppies to her after feeding; she may clean them by licking and encourage their elimination.

Another method used by breeders who have large litters to hand raise is called tube feeding. Before using this method you should talk to your veterinarian and have this technique demonstrated by someone who can show you exactly how to proceed.

Still another way to raise orphan puppies is to find a substitute mother. It need not be a collie. Any breed that will accept the puppies will do. Sometimes a breeder in your area has a dam with puppies or one whose puppies are weaned but who has not dried up. We once needed a substitute mother for a litter. We did not have another dam with puppies, but we did have an older female that had been an exceptional mother and truly loved puppies. We brought her in, thinking she at least would take over the cleaning job. After feeding the puppies we put them in the box with her and she did take care of them. Much to our surprise, within two days, she came into full milk and nursed the litter for three weeks. Apparently this is not an unheard-of event, but it is rather rare.

Responsible Dog Ownership

Good Dog Owner, Good Neighbor

As a dog owner, you know the companionship, loyalty, love, and fun that your dog adds to your life. You also must realize your responsibility toward your neighbors. Dog owners are sometimes insensitive to the barking of their own dog. Put yourself in your neighbors' place to see how your dog's habits affect them. Excessive barking can be extremely annoying!

In a great many areas there are laws written to prohibit a noisy animal within a particular jurisdiction. For example, a typical ordinance might read: "It shall be unlawful for any person to allow prolonged or intense barking or other harsh or excessive noises to be made by any animal under his ownership or control, at any time, so as to disturb the quiet, comfort, or repose of one or more members of the community." It is your responsibility to be familiar with all the laws in your community pertaining to dog ownership.

Barking, of course, can be helpful by alerting owners of potential dangers or warning of a stranger's presence. A barking dog alerts neighbors to intruders when you are not at home, or the dog's barking may indicate an animal in distress.

There are also bad aspects of a barking dog: How will you know if danger is imminent or intruders are present if your dog is allowed to bark over prolonged periods of time for no reason? One dog barking usually starts another dog barking. The noise is aggravating to neighbors, period. They have every right to demand a noise-free environment and you must do everything in your power to drastically reduce the noise. Barking always creates neighborhood arguments and resentments and sometimes leads to warrant citations. It can also be harmful to the dog. This behavior may indicate a bored or highly nervous animal. Unless stopped, barking may develop into a type of hysteria.

You can determine for yourself whether your dog is a good companion and watchdog or a neighborhood noise nuisance.

Unnecessary barking is a nuisance and must be stopped.

A curious collie offers fun and companionship for all ages.

• Determine what causes the dog to bark.
• Be alert to stop the barking as soon as it starts.
• Train your dog to respond to a command to be quiet. Try saying "Enough!" with emphasis.
• Reward your dog whenever it barks for watchdog reasons.
• Don't leave an animal unattended for long periods of time.
• Train your dog to stay quietly within its quarters when you are away.

If you are concerned about a neighbor's barking dog, first try to contact the owner and work out a solution. If this does not work, you have the right to contact your local police department. If you are the owner of such a dog, talk to your neighbors and ask for their patience while you are training your dog. A spirit of cooperation can be created without hard feelings. Tell them you want to know when your dog is disturbing them and assure them you will take care of it. Dogs should be good neighbors, too.

Preventing or breaking a bad habit really depends on you. Remember to reassure your dog by petting it and talking to it when it is quiet and well behaved. It will soon learn that his silence pleases you.

The Importance of the Leash

• The leash is the best birth control device preventing random matings and unwanted puppies.
• It is the best way to keep your dog from injury, keeping your pet from darting into traffic, from dog fights, and encounters with sick or injured wild animals, eliminating pain to the dog and veterinary bills for you.
• It is the best good neighbor policy maker, keeping your pet from any sort of trespassing, destructive or otherwise, on your neighbor's lawn or other private land. It will also keep your pet from jumping up on children or adults

Does your dog bark excessively:
• when someone rings your doorbell?
• when garbage collectors, mail carriers, or paper carriers go past your house?
• when children are playing outside?
• when another animal comes into view?
• when another dog barks?
• when hearing a siren?
• when it wants to get into the house?
• when you leave or return home?
• when left alone?

If your answer is "yes" to any of these questions, your dog probably already is a neighborhood nuisance. This disturbance of the peace is one of the quickest and most common ways to become a bad neighbor. Remember: Persistent barkers are more likely to be ignored if there is a real emergency because they bark all the time.

Fortunately, there are steps you can take:

How much, indeed? All dogs are wonderful, but some make better pets than others. If you have selected a collie you will not be disappointed.

and possibly inflicting injury, fright, or discomfort on them.

- It is the best wildlife and environment protection, keeping your pet from harassing deer and other wild animals, either by himself or as part of a stray dog pack.
- It is the best way to develop an affectionate pet, as the touch of it gives your dog definite assurance that it is protected and loved. Most dogs learn quickly that the leash is a sure sign of an outing with their friend.
- The leash is an extension to the collar. The collar is the best identification service, as the license and rabies tags attached to the collar will get your dog back to you if it should become lost. Use them both as a matter of practice. Check with your local humane society or police department about leash laws in your area.

Useful Addresses and Literature

Useful Addresses

American Veterinary Medical Association
930 North Meacham Road
Schaumberg, IL 60173

American Working Collie Association
Ms. Linda Rorem
1548 Victoria Way
Pacifica, CA 94044

Canine Eye Registration Foundation
South Campus Court, Building C
West Lafayette, IN 47907

Collie Club of America
Carmen Leonard
1119 S. Fleming Road
Woodstock, IL 60098

Collie Club of America Foundation, Inc.
47 Wicks End Lane
Wilton, CT 06897

Orthopedic Foundation for Animals
2300 Nifong Boulevard
Columbia, MO 65201

Therapy Dogs International
P.O. Box 2796
Cheyenne, WY 82203

Kennel Clubs

The American Kennel Club (AKC)
51 Madison Avenue
New York, New York 10010

Australian National Kennel Council
Royal Show Grounds
Ascot Vale
Victoria, Australia

Canadian Kennel Club
89 Skyway Avenue, Suite 100
Etobicoke, Ontario M9W 6R4, Canada

Irish Kennel Club
41 Harcourt Street
Dublin 2, Ireland

New Zealand Kennel Club
P.O. Box 523
Wellington 1, New Zealand

The Kennel Club
1-4 Clargis Street, Picadilly
London W7Y 8AB England

United Kennel Club (UKC)
100 East Kilgore Road
Kalamzoo, Michigan 49001-5598

Useful Books

The following books also are published by Barron's and can be ordered directly from the publisher.

Wrede, B.: *Before You Buy That Puppy,* 1994.
Eldridge, W.: *The Best Pet Name Book Ever,* 1990.
Wrede, B.: *Civilizing Your Puppy,* 1992.
Baer, T.: *Communicating With Your Dog,* 1989.
Klever, U.: *The Complete Book of Dog Care,* 1989.
Alderton, D.: *The Dog Care Manual,* 1986.
Frye, F.: *First Aid for Your Dog,* 1987.
Streitferdt, U.: *Healthy Dog, Happy Dog. A Complete Guide to Dog Diseases and Their Treatment,* 1994.
Baer, T.: *How to Teach Your Old Dog New Tricks,* 1991.

Index

Color photos are indicated in **boldface** type.

Photo Credits

All photos are property of the authors (courtesy *Hawaiian Dog Review* and *Collie Cues*) except: Barbara Eastwood, inside front cover. Rayleen Hendrix, front cover and pp. 5, 13, 31 (top), 36, 48 (middle), 65 (top). Susan Larson, back cover and p. 48 (top). Nancy McDonald (courtesy *Collie Expressions*), pp. 4 (bottom), 8 (bottom), 12, 16 (bottom), 63 (top). Hildegarde Morgan, p. 48 (bottom). Shelley Roos (courtesy *Collie Cues*), p. 26 (top and bottom). Kathy Peters (courtesy *Collie Cues*), p. 89. M. Sullivan, back cover (courtesy *Collie Expressions*).

Cover Photos

Front cover: Proud mother and eager puppy.
Inside front cover: Blue merle male pup.
Inside back cover: The handsome features of a stud dog.
Back cover: Collies are great with children, but face licking should be discouraged (top left). Mother with three-week-old puppies (top right). Tricolor and sable rough collies (bottom left). Herding instinct testing (bottom right).

All inquiries should be addressed to:
Barron's Educational Series, Inc.
250 Wireless Boulevard
Hauppauge, New York 11788

Library of Congress Catalog Card No. 94-72141
International Standard Book No. 0-8120-1875-3

PRINTED IN HONG KONG

567   9927   987

BARRON'S PET REFERENCE BOOKS

Barron's Pet Reference Books are and have long been the choice of experts and discerning pet owners. Why? Here are just a few reasons. These indispensable volumes are packed with 35 to 200 stunning full-color photos. Each provides the very latest expert information and answers questions that pet owners often wonder about.

BARRON'S PET REFERENCE BOOKS ARE:

AQUARIUM FISH
AQUARIUM FISH BREEDING
THE AQUARIUM FISH SURVIVAL MANUAL
AQUARIUM PLANTS MANUAL
BEFORE YOU BUY THAT KITTEN
BEFORE YOU BUY THAT PUPPY
THE BEST PET NAME BOOK EVER
THE COMPLETE BOOK OF BUDGERIGARS
CARING FOR YOUR OLDER CAT
CARING FOR YOUR OLDER DOG
CARING FOR YOUR SICK CAT
THE CAT CARE MANUAL
CIVILIZING YOUR PUPPY
COMMUNICATING WITH YOUR DOG
THE COMPLETE BOOK OF CAT CARE
THE COMPLETE BOOK OF DOG CARE
THE COMPLETE BOOK OF PARAKEET CARE
THE DOG CARE MANUAL
EDUCATING YOUR DOG
THE EXOTIC PET SURVIVAL MANUAL

FEEDING YOUR PET BIRD
FUN AND GAMES WITH YOUR DOG
GOLDFISH AND ORNAMENTAL CARP
GUIDE TO A WELL-BEHAVED CAT
GUIDE TO A WELL-BEHAVED PARROT
GUIDE TO HOME PET GROOMING
HAND-FEEDING AND RAISING BABY BIRDS
HEALTHY CAT, HAPPY CAT
HEALTHY DOG, HAPPY DOG
HOP TO IT: A Guide To Training Your Pet Rabbit
THE HORSE CARE MANUAL
HOW TO TEACH YOUR OLD DOG NEW TRICKS
INDOOR CATS
LABYRINTH FISH
LIZARD CARE FROM A TO Z
NONVENOMOUS SNAKES
THE SECRET LIFE OF CATS
SHOW ME
THE ULTRAFIT OLDER CAT
THE TROPICAL MARINE FISH SURVIVAL MANUAL

Barron's Educational Series, Inc., 250 Wireless Boulevard, Hauppauge, New York 11788. For sales information call toll-free: 1-800-645-3476.

In Canada: Georgetown Book Warehouse, 34 Armstrong Avenue, Georgetown, Ontario L7G 4R9. Call toll-free: 1-800-247-7160.
Order from your favorite bookstore or pet shop.

(#64) R 2/97